NOT BUSINESS AS USUAL
MATT DANSWAN

Ark House Press
PO Box 1722, Port Orchard, WA 98366 USA
PO Box 1321, Mona Vale NSW 1660 Australia
PO Box 318 334, West Harbour, Auckland 0661 New Zealand
arkhousepress.com

© 2018 Matt Danswan

All rights reserved. No part of this publication may be reproduced, stored in a retrieval system or transmitted in any form or by any means electronic, mechanical, photocopying, recording or otherwise without the prior written permission of the publisher.

Cataloguing in Publication Data:
Title: Not Business As Usual
ISBN: 9780995421585 (pbk.)
Subjects: Biography; Christian; Business;
Other Authors/Contributors: Danswan, Matt; Danswan, Nicole

Design and layout by initiateagency.com

Matt Danswan is man who has displayed determination, resilience, insight and foresight within his professional business career which has enabled him to be successful over many decades, in a number of industries. But his greatest achievements are not the result of business acumen, but of his character. His family, friends and those fortunate to know him are the beneficiaries of his loving, compassionate, empathetic and generous nature. He is a leader in every way.

Ward Lucas
Senior Pastor of C3 Rozelle, Sydney Australia

When going into business or friendships I look for three qualities, honesty, passion and an ability to listen. Matt Danswan carries all these characters plus more! A devoted dad and husband, Matt juggles his love of entrepreneurial visions and his faith and always combines both to create the best outcomes for all! I'm lucky I've experienced both, but will always put my friendship with Matt and his family as a priority!

Matt Adamson
Former Rugby League International
State of Origin representative
Fox Sports and Channel 7 TV personality

I have known Matt Danswan for more than eight years. In this time I have found him to be a man enriched with passion, commitment and encouragement, with Christ always at the centre of whatever he does.

Tim Pascoe
Director, Tim Pascoe Photography

Matt Danswan, who I have known for 20 years, is not only an entrepreneur of all sorts, but a man that sticks to his guns and shows integrity when wise decisions need to be made under heated circumstances.

When you need someone to be on the front line with you in battle, just call on Matt. He will be right by your side.

Peter Kelaher,
Director, PK Property Byers Agents, Sydney Australia

Matthew Danswan, a friend of mine for over 40 years! Throughout our lives he has been an inspiring person with his excellent conversational skills, contagious approach to living and his willingness to become all god has created him to be in every facet of his life. He continues to achieve goals that many just dream. This book will be a great tool for those looking to develop their lives, family and businesses, God's way.

Glenn Wysman
Friend and Pastor of The Link Church, Sydney Australia

"NOT Business As Usual" perfectly describes Matt Danswan and his approach to life and business. As long as I've known Matt I've seen him display out-of-the-box thinking, mixed with God-seeking wisdom and as a result he and his amazing wife/business partner Nicole have built not only a great business, but also enviable lives. He and Nicole live well balanced, Christ-centered lives and are great examples of Christians who choose to succeed in all they do and be blessings to all they meet.

I believe this book will be a great blessing to anyone called into business and those seeking an alternative to the 'cookie cutter' business models employed by most.

Christian McCudden
Lead Pastor, C3 Noosa

If you feel like your work life and your Christian life aren't working together, this is the book to read.

Matt's refreshing and inspiring real-life story is an eye opener for today's current and aspiring entrepreneurs, bringing new ideas and how to bring God into your business.

I personally feel this book will make a difference in the way you do business.

Nick Georgas
Director, New York Wings

Matt Danswan is, to put it bluntly, one of the good guys. A man of great faith and great energy, he has a knack for seeing things differently. For him NOT business as usual is, in fact, business as usual if that makes sense. I have benefited often from his enthusiasm, passion and sharpness of insight. I have no doubt that anyone who takes a leaf out of his book (pun intended!) will be greatly blessed!

Berni Dymet
CEO of Christianityworks

DEDICATION

This book is dedicated to my family. That is all-encompassing. To my immediate family: my wife Nicole, my four children, Morgan, Ava, Hayden and Imogen – you guys rock my world... and you make it all worthwhile.

I want to also take this opportunity to thank my parents. My Mum has been such a rock in my life and spends hours in prayer for our business. Her love and sacrifice over the years I cannot thank enough for. She is also a part of our team at Initiate Media and is so valued.

My Dad, who sadly passed away in 2016, was one of the wisest men I have ever met. He showed me the way, and he has left me (hopefully) able to do the same for my family. Dad, I hope to leave the same legacy for my children that you left for me.

My sister Nicolle has been an amazing support for me. We are very close and have been through a lot together. Thank you for your friendship and love. It simply means so much.

Back to my wife. I simply could not do it without this amazing woman. She and I make the best team, both as business and life partners. Her mental strength is just phenomenal. She really is the calm in the storm. Nothing fazes her, and nothing keeps her up at night. She doesn't hold on to possessions or anything of this world too tightly, so nothing causes her too much worry. She is the ultimate 'Proverbs 31' woman.

They say that behind every great man is a great woman. This woman is beyond great. She is the love of my life and without her I would honestly not be able to do what I do. Thank you. Thank you. Thank you.

CONTENTS

Dedication — vii
Introduction — xi

1. My Parallels With Surfing — 1
2. A Dreamer Never Sleeps — 17
3. The Surf Lifestyle — 25
4. Grandma's Genes — 43
5. Compounding Interest — 51
6. First Attempts — 61
7. Time To Get Serious — 75
8. The Chicken Roll Transformation — 85
9. Hitting The Wall — 99
10. Time To Clear My Debts — 109
11. The World Of Publishing — 119
12. The No Debt Strategy — 131
13. Finding Synergy — 137
14. Counting The Cost — 151
15. When Publishing Hit The Wall — 159
16. I Need A Breakthrough — 169
17. Final Thoughts — 181
18. Journeying Together — 185

The Entrepreneur's Wife — 189

INTRODUCTION

Life is an interesting journey – and it's even more interesting when you let God take the reins. *NOT Business As Usual* is such a story. I feel like I have lived a life of absolute faith; pure trust in God to build a business that, in the natural, was not there to be built. If it was, then it was not readily apparent that there was even a commercial market for it. That market is Christian media.

Most people go into a business with solid facts and figures behind them of the industry they are proposing to enter. Take fast food as an example. You want to launch a new burger chain and so you do the math. The fast food market in the USA, as of 2018, is forecast to reach $210 billion in sales. So based on this, there is a market share that you can work your business plan or model around. You could say that you want to get a four percent market share, and based on 2018 forecasts, you could have a business that is doing $7.64 billion in annual revenue. At least in theory!

Why Christian media?

I never had the desire to be in the Christian marketplace. Like most Christian business people, I felt my role was to be in the mainstream market, using my success to help bring funds into the ministry and mission areas. Being in the mainstream marketplace was where I started out. That was where I was comfortable, and I was never intimidated by being in the business world. I always found people to be people, and by and large, people in the business world honest to deal with. If you had a product or service they wanted, then they were prepared to pay for it. Yes, it's dog eat dog, but it's also supply and demand, and if you have a good product or service, then the market would demand it from you, the supplier. It's survival of the fittest, so if you're good enough – or you have a good enough product or service – then you can make it. It really is pretty simple.

Interestingly, many people in ministry are perceived to be in Christian work because they are looking for an easier life (the perception being that ministry is hidden away from the 'real world', thus making it comfortable, easy and to some, a bit of a crutch). But it is probably the polar opposite. In building Initiate Media, I have never worked harder. The mainstream world has a river of money flowing. In every industry, as I mentioned above, there is a market cap, and every day around the world these industries have billions of dollars globally flowing through them. The Christian marketplace certainly has the same, but it is not as defined. You cannot just walk in, set up shop, and see business waltz through the door, as you could if you set up a café, a hamburger shop or a local real estate office.

But when it comes to ministry work, it is totally different. There is no such defined 'industry'. In the case of churches, they are completely reliant on tithes and offerings. Missions, or charities, as they are better known as in the mainstream marketplace, also rely on the generosity of others to support their work through donations, and while so do mainstream missions, they do have access to a much greater pool of people. We also have Christian retailers, but, again, there is no access to bestsellers like *Fifty Shades of Gray* and Harry Potter, books that can literally prop up the average store. Only recently I read that Jeff Kinney's series *Diary of a Wimpy Kid* had sold over 150 million copies. We also don't have books by all the major sports stars and entertainers, let alone all the blockbuster movies.

So being in the Christian industry is far from easy. Of course, we hear a lot of noise about those in the Christian market who really make it. From Hillsong, to Joyce Meyer, Rick Warren and Joel Osteen. Sure, there are some big names who have made millions, but really, in a business sense, these are the 'Rupert Murdochs', the 'Steve Jobs', the 'Warren Buffetts' and the 'Bill Gates' of their market. In other words, they are the 'category-killers'; the one percent who have achieved results that the average ministry could never even dream of.

Speaking of those pastors, surely there is the opportunity for us in Christian media to publish their books? Great thought! However the Christian book, music and movie market has caught the eye of Hollywood media moguls and New York publishing houses. It might surprise you to know that Rupert Murdoch, through his book publishing business Harper Collins, owns Thomas Nelson and Zondervan, the two largest Christian book publishers in the world. The French publisher Hachette owns FaithWords, which counts Joyce Meyer, Joel Osteen and John Maxwell among its authors, and the other majors like Baker House, Multnomoah and so on are all under Random House, another global media giant owned by the German company Bertelsmann Media. Simon & Schuster, a division of the media giant CBS Corporation, also owns Howard Books.

Even the children's favorite, 'VeggieTales' is now owned by DreamWorks Animation. Music is mostly through Word Entertainment or Sony Provident, and most faith-based movies are distributed through the major Hollywood studios. None of this is wrong or immoral, I might add; it merely proves that the one part of the Christian market that is truly lucrative – publishing and distribution – is largely owned by the world's major secular media companies.

That said, it is still a marketplace that does $5 billion in the US in annual sales, so I am not crying poor, just merely pointing out that it is not a clearly defined industry and so not easy to derive revenue from.

So the Christian marketplace or ministry is not easy! If God calls you to it, you'll need to count the cost, as there is a lot you may also go without. The people in this market work easily as hard as anyone else, but we don't have as big a pool of revenue.

A Heart After God

God's ways are different to the world's and as such we need to think differently. But mostly, I believe that the doors that have opened for me are due to just wanting to see God's kingdom expand. God is looking for people who can help Him grow His kingdom. The harvest is plentiful, but the workers are few (Matthew 9:37), and as such if you want to see great things happen, then simply wanting to serve Him is where it all starts from. With that servant heart, God can do anything with you.

I remember hearing a preacher telling the story of a young man who was assigned to look after him for the days he was attending a particular church to speak at their conference. The young man was to pick him up from the airport, drive him to and from his hotel, and generally be the go-to person for any needs he may have while he was in the church's care.

The preacher told the story about how passionate the young man was. From meeting him at the airport, to opening the door for him, taking care of his bags, and ensuring his every need was met, the preacher was impressed with the enthusiasm that the young man showed. Given this preacher did this for many weeks of the year and was cared for by many similar church members doing pretty much the same service, he was well placed to see that this young man really stood out.

The young man is now one of the world's most successful itinerant preachers. His name is John Bevere, and as of today John Bevere would also be one of the world's bestselling Christian authors. So it starts at the bottom. The heart you have for serving God and the church could have a massive impact on what you may be doing in the years to come.

Time and again I have seen people who want to see great things happen in their lives, but they don't have God's way. It's easy to want to be at the top, but it starts at the bottom. It also takes commitment to prayer, reading and general time with God to really hear from Him on what He is calling you to do, and to also get that God perspective on the way He wants you to do it. Remember, this is *NOT Business As Usual.* If you have the ability to be patient, to seek Him and to move with His calling, then absolutely anything is possible for you.

It's not how you start, but how you finish
Everyone has a unique journey. A pastor, author, speaker and

good friend of mine is likewise a great example of not only God at work, but also how God uses people from such different backgrounds. His book is based on an underground upbringing. He tells the story of a life of crime, pretty much raised on the streets of Melbourne, Australia. In Australia we have had a very successful television series that ran for several years called 'Underbelly'. It has been a major ratings success, as the average Australian, with no links to crime and drugs (that we know of...) gets an inside glimpse of the 'underbelly' world that lurks just beneath the surface of every major city.

The first series was based around the drug families and ganglands of Melbourne. It featured the likes of the Moran family and a very well known guy by the name of Carl Williams. Interestingly, as I write this, all of the 'stars' of the show (and I use that term loosely) have been murdered. The last of the Morans, Des Moran, was shot and killed while drinking coffee outside a Melbourne café. While the most famous, Carl Williams, died in 2010 in prison, where he was struck in the back of the head with the stem of an exercise bike. Interestingly because the footage was caught on CCV cameras, we Australians were shown the single blow on TV that killed him.

My friend grew up with these same Melbourne crime figures, but a twist in his life meant that he met the Lord before he had a chance to really get into the world that they were in. His upbringing is so different – and so far away – from mine that it is not funny, but this just points to the way God uses different people for different works. He is touching and reaching people that I could never. He has rehabilitation centers, pastors a church in the tough, working class Melbourne western suburbs, and he ministers to people that someone like me never could.

Like my friend, God will take your history and your life – good and bad – to carve something out that will bring Him glory. It is His specialty. He is the master at using the most unusual people to do the most amazing work. As my wife always says, "It's not how you start, it's how you finish," so start with what you've got.

Another brief example is of a man called David Bussau. David Bussau founded a charity called Opportunity International. Coming from a tough upbringing, he heard the call of God, heeded it, and then started an organization that does some amazing work. Opportunity International specializes in providing micro-finance (small loans) in some of the world's poorest countries. Working along the lines that it is better to give someone a hand up as opposed to a hand out, his organization loans the money to individuals who want and desire to start a business.

Each person must qualify for the loan, however, and then must stick to the payment schedule. Interestingly, they have a very small number of loans that default, showing that those who apply for – and are granted a loan – honor this commitment.

In 2003 David won the 'Ernst & Young Entrepreneur of the Year' award, which is a highly prestigious award that many in business would dearly desire to win. Also, running a not-for-profit made David a first. I was not at the awards night, but according to a friend who was, David Bussau stunned the crowd as he gave his acceptance speech. As the emcee asked him about his business: how he plans, how he looks ahead etc, the crowd was amazed as David told them that he does not rely on one, five and ten year business plans, but that He trusts God, listens to God, and then does what God tells Him to do. There is no set plan in place!

Now in business, goal setting and planning forward are badges of honor, and anyone who doesn't would be laughed at. How can you run an organization – either for profit or non-profit – that does not have sufficient planning in place? And while I am a big fan of planning, I go straight to Proverbs 19:21:

"Many are the plans in a person's heart, but it is the Lord's purpose that prevails."

So planning is good, goal setting is great, and knowing where you want to go is essential, but daily those plans need to be 'washed' against God's plans for your life. Don't set them in stone; leave room for God to carve out His own plans.

If there is anything I want you to take out of this book, it is that God can do anything. I have penned this book for you, not me. I have agonized for years about telling my story, as I don't like publicity. So if any part of this book feels like I am beating my chest as I write it, I can tell you the opposite is the case. Flashing your story and life around on Instagram might be the way the Millennials live, but I'm a bit more old school than that. I love privacy and have always loved being anonymous. However, this book is to help show you that all things are possible with God. Standing up for your faith – and putting your face to it – takes some courage, but someone's got to do it, so when I felt God ask me to, I was brave enough to say *yes*.

So as you read this book, my prayer is that it awakens the giant that is within you. I know this is a phrase from Anthony Robbins, and all credit to him, but in reality, there is a giant within you.

There is the God who owns the sheep on a thousand hills, and there is nothing He cannot do. The key is to get inspiration from others, benchmark off other people and businesses, but then stay within your calling. Stick with what you're good at, skilled at, and where you think God may have placed your anointing. Your talents are generally a great pointer as to where your calling lies.

Don't copy someone else's calling. Admire them and learn from them, but don't be envious of them. You can't do something amazing when you're simply watching and copying other people. So get out there and do something awesome with the one life you've got. Aim to live a life where people will be inspired by you, rather than simply trying to be like other people. I am cheering on from the sidelines for you.

… And remember, it's not how you start, it's how you finish.

If there were dreams to sell, what would you buy!
THOMAS LOVELL BEDDOES

CHAPTER ONE

MY PARALLELS WITH SURFING

You will find as you read this book that surfing has played a pretty major part in my life, and it still does. I am in the water at leat three times per week. I liken surfing to business. The ocean is a very dangerous place, capable on the right day of taking a person's life with ease. Yet the experienced surfer avoids so much punishment from the ocean by not only respecting it, but also learning how to navigate its dangers.

Knowing when to paddle out, when to start scratching for the horizon; knowing what waves to take off on, or not. This knowledge can literally be the difference between life and death in bigger surf. Or at least in a not so dramatic example, the difference between a major beating or a triumphant outcome.

I occasionally watch a reality TV show in Australia called 'Bondi Rescue', where the show follows the life and times of the lifeguards at Australia's most famous beach, and I wonder how people can get the ocean so wrong. These people get into all sorts of trouble, whilst much of the time the ocean isn't even raging or close to its angriest when they do. It's a pretty simple city beach, with red and yellow flags patrolled by lifeguards, which indicate the safest place to swim. So it is with business. At one end of the scale we have billionaires living the dream, swanning around in places like Monaco or the Bahamas, or Palm Beach, Florida. Yet at the other end we have bankruptcy, liquidation and foreclosures and lives – and often marriages and families – in turmoil because of business failings. How can a few get it so right and the others so wrong?

A good surfer is a trained surfer. They are trained for all conditions. Yet further to this, they never just arrived at the beach and paddled out in a life-threatening ocean. No, they started as kids. They learnt all the basic skills on small waves close to shore. As they advanced in their skills and gained strength, they took on bigger waves so by the time they are surfing dangerous conditions, they are physically and mentally prepared. What is life-threatening to the general public is more than manageable for them because they are trained.

My boys are both surfers. When they were very young they started paddling their foam surfboards in the rock pool at the beach. Once they felt comfortable paddling the boards and trying to stand up, we then left that pool and moved into the ocean. But we always surfed at low tide so they could walk in and out of the shallows, all the while practicing paddling for and standing up on waves. At the same time they were doing swimming lessons to ensure they would be competent in the ocean in the years to come.

My 9 year-old now jumps off the rocks with me when we surf

the point breaks, as he has slowly progressed to the point where he can handle surfing across rocks.

Business is not much different. If you leave the safety of a company you have worked in for 20 years, and with no overall experience in the running of a business, start loading your business up with overheads and expenses, there is every chance you'll be one of the people in bankruptcy. More likely it will be this, as opposed to those swanning around in Majorca. However if you start small, take your time and learn as you go, then you will slowly be able to take on more risk.

Entrepreneurs don't like the word 'slow'. However the opposite to this is 'fast', and the danger in growing too fast is that it is… dangerous. When your business starts exceeding your skill level, you run the risk of serious problems. So while we all like to have the trappings of a successful business, our biggest challenge is that we don't race to this point, get that car and office we've always wanted, only to find our business doesn't yet have the foundations, or we don't yet have the business skills, and it is all going to be all over sometime soon.

In fact, I often wonder what would happen if God gave us all we prayed for when we asked Him for it. Most of us would make an absolute mess of our lives because we aren't trained to manage this. So if you liken business to surfing, you'll soon see why you have to take your time in developing the competence it takes to build a bigger and bigger business.

If you agree to read this book, then one thing is non-negotiable: you must be willing to think outside the square. That is a prerequisite. The business world is changing fast and accordingly we must be open to new ways of doing business. As

Isaiah 55:8 says:

> *"For my thoughts are not your thoughts, neither are your ways my ways."*

A Harvard MBA graduate might not like or agree with my model, but that's okay. That's why it is written in an autobiographical style. It's my model, it has worked for me, and you can feel to pick and choose as you feel necessary the parts that might work for you.

God's ways will already contradict the world's, and therefore if you're feeling like He is showing you a way that is different to the way the world does it, then it just might be God giving you your own *NOT Business As Usual* strategy.

On the record when it comes to money and giving

In life they say there are three things that you should not discuss: money, politics and religion. So we are immediately breaking that rule in discussing two of them side by side because there has been a lot of diverse teaching in the church on money, leaving most Christians a bit baffled on the subject.

Straight up, I'd really love to give you my insight on being a Christian in business and where I stand on money (and the church). So immediately you're either going to like my stance and you're going to want to read on, or you're going to read these next couple of pages and slam the book down, disagreeing with my philosophy – or theology – surrounding money. I am hoping it's the former, but if it's the latter… Well, at least we got this far. So here goes:

I have been in the church my entire life, and so the whole area of 'does God want us to be rich/poor/have just enough?' for our existence or survival is one I have personally had many years to think about. I've also had a lot of time to pray about it for my own life, allowing me to make decisions as to how I think my life and its finances should be managed. Firstly, I think the Bible contains a number of 'grey' areas. These areas we need to think out for ourselves. Of course there are things like The Ten Commandments and loving God with all your heart, loving your neighbor, and so on that are non-negotiables. They are not grey, but rather black and white.

But outside of that, there are many parts to our lives where God gives us a freewill and we are free to make personal decisions as to the direction we should take. Take two examples here:

"The borrower is the slave to the lender." Proverbs 22:7

"You shall lend to many nations, but borrow from none." Deuteronomy 15:6

Neither of these scriptures are commandments; they are more suggestions on how you should live your life. If you buy five investment properties, each financed by the bank, I don't think God's going to turn you away from eternity on Judgment Day! This is why as we seek out God and His Word: He reveals things to us. So on we go.

Over the last number of years I believe we have basically seen three key financial teachings on money, with Christians tending to choose one that they align with.

1. The Prosperity Doctrine

The crux of this doctrine is two-fold. Firstly, God wants you to be exceedingly rich. Sadly the world seems to believe this is what all Pentecostal churches are pushing and some high profile pastors have abused this for their own benefit. Secondly, at the lower end of this doctrine is the belief that God wants to bless your life so you can bless others. As one of His children, He has blessings for us (including financial ones) that he wants to pour out into our lives.

A popular verse used to support this doctrine is *"Give, and it will be given to you. A good measure, pressed down, shaken together and running over, will be poured into your lap. For with the measure you use, it will be measured to you."* (Luke 6:38)

This scripture is almost always used in terms of 'financial gain' instead of applying it to all facets of your life.

2. The Poverty Doctrine

While it is not called this as such, this belief is that as Jesus had nothing, we should have nothing. There are people right around the world unable to feed themselves, and so it is wrong for the Christian to store up his/her treasures on earth. The scripture pointed to in this instance is Matthew 6:19. We are to pick up our Cross, essentially left to suffer through life because a) we shouldn't be storing up our treasures on earth, and b) we cannot take any of it with us anyway.

3. The 'Just-Enough' Doctrine

This is the 'God will supply my needs, not wants' doctrine. God won't give you more than you need; he'll supply what you need to make it through, but any more and you might start worshipping money. The detractors of this doctrine state that how can we help others if we are flat out paying our own bills?

So I would say, from my perspective, these are the three general doctrines out there that most Christians fall into if we were to interview a cross-section of people. The alternative might be that the subject of money is taboo because it is never discussed or taught in church. Therefore, many people have no view, as there is no teaching on the subject. In this case, the less said the better.

If I had to choose one of those three doctrines to live my financial life within, I guess that I could fall into the first, except that I am dead against the idea of us needing God Himself to make us rich. The Prosperity Doctrine has caused Christians to take an absolute beating in the mainstream world and those preachers have been held up as the trophy holders of this doctrine, and accordingly the church – and its attendees – have copped a battering. This prosperity doctrine has also caused a lot of people to walk away from God when they have not received the financial blessing that they were 'promised'. As such the word 'prosperity' is now a dirty word in the church.

Now I would like to suggest that there is a fourth doctrine and probably the one that I subscribe to. This is what I would like to call, **The Blessing of God Doctrine**. Not making us rich, **as we can do that ourselves**, if we have the desire – but having a blessing and favor on us as His children. For us to not believe that we are any different from the world is totally wrong. In fact, that old bumper sticker that says, 'Christians aren't perfect, just forgiven' is missing a whole lot of truth. Essentially it is telling the world that, "Hey, I'm actually exactly the same as you. The only difference with you and I is that my sins are forgiven and yours are not."

What a false doctrine. You mean that having the Holy Spirit in your life, having a wisdom that only comes from God – a wisdom that is reserved for *His* people – makes me exactly the same as everyone else in the world? I don't think so. I have the God who created this entire world as my Father. I have His mind, (1 Corinthians 2:16) and I have His favor (Proverbs 3:4).

Personally, I understand where many of these preachers are coming from. They have stepped out in faith in their own lives, and many people don't give them credit for the size of the organizations they are responsible for. They have multi-million dollar budgets, hundreds of staff on their payroll – and it all has to be funded by tithes and offerings. So these guys have stepped out on the promises of God – and seen God's supernatural provision – and now they believe that others can too.

Don't get me wrong; there are definitely pastors who take the Word out of context and have done much damage in their prosperity doctrine. I am certainly not here to defend those who have crossed the line and made the Bible all about money or success. However, going to the other end of the spectrum is not the answer either. We then have all these under-achieving Christians in our midst and we miss influencing the world in the marketplace. This is where I believe the church has fallen into a massive hole, and we are no longer the influencers in our society.

This **Blessing of God Doctrine**, I believe, is that we have the blessing and favor of God on our lives as heirs to the Kingdom. This blessing is reserved for God's people, however, where I have an issue is that some preachers never explain *how* their church members could get rich. To this day I just cannot get how tipping larger and larger offerings into a plate can make you rich - if you're then going to go home and live your life the same way you always have.

To me that is really treating God like He is a lottery. Based on this you'd give as much as you could, like you're putting in more money into a high-yield investment to get a greater return. You give, and God does all the work for you. So again, where this falls over in my mind is when people in roles that do not allow them to advance in pay (take teachers, nurses, truck drivers, restaurant workers and so on) are asked to give over and above, in the hope they will gain more. So over the years I have seen many people disillusioned by continually giving, yet years later, their financial worlds really have not changed.

Sure, we need to support the local church, and that I truly believe in. But there is a point where if the individual does not do something different in their lives, then there is a very good chance that their financial life may look no different some years from now. Other than capital gain on home ownership, this may be the only way that a person sees any increase for all their hard work.

Conversely, I don't believe in **The Poverty Doctrine**, where we need to take a vow of poverty, or on a lesser scale, have nothing to show for our hard work. Whether we like it or not, we live in a world run by money. I didn't choose it to be that way, you didn't choose this, and neither did the church. This is the way our economy – and world – operates. So money is a major part of our lives, whether we like it or not. We cannot get away from this fact, and so trying to separate church and money, or the Christian and money, is simply not possible. Money, to a large degree, rules our lives. If you disagree with this, then I would ask you: Did you get out of bed this morning and trudge off to work? Unless it's a weekend, then you probably did, because you *need* money. And God actually supplies your needs through this work.

But the Bible clearly says that *"The love of money is the root of all evil"* (Timothy 6:10); and *"It is difficult for the rich man to enter the kingdom of God…"* (Matthew 19:16-24) Can I tell you from personal experience that I have always 'loved' money way more when I haven't had it than when I have. When I'm down to my last dollar, or work is quiet, or I'm facing bills that are mounting in my life, I love money so much more because I *need* it. I also love it more when the offering basket comes around at church because that is money I need to survive! It takes every inch of my faith to instead give it to God.

But when times are good and I am not having to be so tight with it, that is when I have the control over it, and so it flows out of my life with ease. I remember a preacher once saying that some people are so tight with their money that there are tears coming out of the faces on the notes (of the money) they are holding. A great little analogy.

I also note in Matthew 19:23 that it is 'difficult', or 'harder' for someone to enter the kingdom of God. It did not say 'impossible', yet we have held up this passage of scripture like a trophy, pointing to it as though it is *not possible*. The Bible does not say that, yet we interpret it that way. It is essentially saying that if you have money, your needs are met, and thus you don't feel like you have the need to have God in your life, then it will be harder for you to enter the kingdom of God. That is because most people come to God in times of need. When times are good, who needs God? You're 'self-made' and with this generally comes self pride. So the man or woman with adequate supply finds it harder to have God in his or her life because being self-made often means being full of pride too.

Category three is a category that I believe is not only selfish, but also allows its believers to wash their hands of any responsibility with their money. Peter Daniels, a business speaker, wrote a really interesting book some years ago called *How to be Happy Though Rich*. It's an intriguing title, as of course you'd be happy if you were rich, right?

But he makes a really valid argument. Peter suggests that with wealth comes great responsibility, and so it is very easy to sit back and criticize those with money, without realizing that those who have it actually also have a lot more responsibility in their lives than those who don't. In fact it helped change my life.

If you want to be 'rich', as the prosperity preacher might say, then he might also need to add that in doing so you're going to have to own a business, or have a stressful high-end corporate job, meaning you're taking on lots more hours, responsibility and stress, or you may have a major property or investment portfolio that you need to preserve. Or you'll need to be a top sportsperson or entertainer, and both of those occupations, while being high paid, are also high stress due to the lack of certainty and having to constantly perform at your peak. For when we look around the world at the 'rich', unless it is inherited money, most are living very difficult, challenging lives; lives of great responsibility. And did I mention risk? We haven't even got to the fact that many of them struggle to sleep because of the responsibilities that they carry. For most, great wealth is born out of great risk. With risk comes reward.

So if it is more money you want, then I challenge you to likewise be ready for greater headaches. You might also need to switch the TV off and spend more time reading, studying, watching seminars or experts on Youtube to learn more about the field you want to move into.

The women's magazines will make it look like all of Hollywood is swanning around in the Caribbean on holidays living an easy life, when in reality that would only be one percent of that entire movie and entertainment industry. Really, only sportspeople and entertainers – and there are only a few of them – are the ones paid the ridiculously big money without the ridiculously big (financial) risk. For everyone else, there is lots of risk that goes into every dollar they make. Please, do know I am not saying here that entertainers and sports starts don't work hard and take risks. Go with me on the overall point I am making.

In the process of being supposedly rich, you also have lots of extra responsibilities. From additional taxation issues and challenges of where to invest, complicated tax returns that account for all your investments, staff that you are responsible for (all of whom have rent or mortgage commitments and families reliant on that weekly income) and being a good steward of that bigger investment is a responsibility that many don't want. So does God want you to be rich? I am going to answer my ultimate take on this by asking you the question: Do you want to be rich? You're the one who will decide on the answer, not God. If you have the ideas, the work ethic, and then the strong stomach to go through the ups and downs of accumulating money, then, yes, you can be as rich as you like. The world is literally your oyster!

If you're happy for the additional workload, responsibility and stress that comes with it, then there is no limit on how far you can go or on how much money you can make. The call is ultimately yours, as you're in control of how you live your life, what you do/want to do for a living, and then how you spend your money. You – and only you – will ultimately decide if you're rich or not. And then only you can decide if you end up 'worshipping' your money, or whether you become tight-fisted with it and only choose to do as you wish with it. Or you might give it all away, knowing that because you have the skills to make more, you don't need to be so tight-fisted with it.

While I am aware that this sounds a little self righteous, I have never lived my life just for money. I live my life to live out my goals, to use all the talents that God has given me, and whether that makes me rich, comfortable, or still not quite there, that's what gets me out of bed. Of course, being in business, it's natural that you get a high out of signing deals, bringing in new orders and watching your turnover - and profit - increase. But I have personally found that you don't need to worship money to make money. If you're good at what you do, the money will naturally come.

Business is basic supply and demand, so as long as you have a product or service that the market wants, and you think you can market it better or in a different way to your competitors, then the money is there to be had. Simple, really.

Finally, I also firmly believe that we only have one shot at this life. We have each been fearfully and wonderfully made, and as such you have one go to make a difference. Proverbs 10:4 says, *"Lazy hands make for poverty, but diligent hands bring wealth."*

So coming back to Peter Daniels's book, how much money you make is up to you, not God, and not the prosperity preacher. But it's then your responsibility to steward it.

If only life was easy!

Being a business owner and having the ability to employ other people, which in turn feeds families, puts a roof over their heads, and ultimately sees people raise a family, is no light calling. Being an employer is, in my opinion and experience, one of the biggest responsibilities a person will have. It's also a ministry in its own right. Creating work for the community is a major deal. It's right up there with the responsibility of raising children – and again in my opinion, is probably harder.

I'll end now as this is not a book on money, but faith and business. Hopefully though I have set the platform for my beliefs – whether you believe they are good, bad or otherwise. Be excellent at what you do, work hard, invest, and over time, you'll find that you can do pretty well financially for yourself.

So are you reading on, or have I offended you and you're about to hit social media to advise people not to read this book? The choice is yours, and that's the risk one takes when they decide to take their thoughts and put them down on paper. Anyway, it's probably why I would have preferred to remain anonymous. Hopefully we can continue on from here…

When you cease to dream you cease to live.
MALCOLM FORBES

CHAPTER TWO

A DREAMER NEVER SLEEPS

"You shall lend to many nations, but borrow from none." Deuteronomy 15:6

You may know the above scripture. Interestingly, it is a way to live, and not a command from God. If it were, then we may have had the Eleven Commandments. The Bible is full of wisdom; ways that we can live our lives that add value to our days. But not one word of this wisdom do we have to follow. We all have the option of doing as we like.

God has given each of us a freewill and as such we can all live our lives as we choose. The Bible was written as the guideline for our Christian walk. Think of God as your life or business coach, or even personal trainer. You are the 'owner' of your life on this earth, and you have been given a freewill. Your life is yours to do with as you wish. So as a Christian, really it is up to you how much of the Bible's 'advice' you choose to live by.

I can go to my personal trainer (if I had one…) and he/she can give me a rundown of what my life needs to look like to be in the best shape, plus keep my insides healthy so that as I age, I do it in the best possible condition. I can pay them to roll out a plan for what my life looks like daily in terms of the sleep I get, the exercise I should do, and the foods I should consume. Together we can create a great plan for my life. Then I can leave our meeting, fitness and diet plans in hand, and do as I wish.

Then I can come back to this same person some months later to report on my condition. They can either take one look at me and see I have followed their advice, or they can size me up and realize that I decided to do my own thing. Ultimately I am the one responsible for my life and I cannot blame the trainer for my failings.

So it is when we come to the way you run your business or manage your life's affairs. It's your business or your life, so you have the control. These are not 'heaven and hell' choices that are on the line here. They are your choices. However, that does not always mean that you're going to make the right decisions. So the better the people you surround yourself with – God and His Word included – hopefully the better results you will achieve.

The importance of planning

One of my strengths in business is planning. I don't believe we get to where we are meant to go in life simply by letting the wind drift us along. In Australia, we have red and yellow flags at the beach to determine the designated area to swim between. This is the area that the lifeguards patrol and deem to be the safest for the general public. I have found that if I go to the beach for a swim and jump in the water, invariably there is a slight current that is pulling gently to the left or the right, even if it looks calm from the shore. The ocean never stops moving. If you're not concentrating on what you are doing, it doesn't take long until you have drifted from where you are meant to be (that is, between the flags).

So it is with life. If there is no plan, no true north to where you are heading, then you are just drifting, being pulled from one direction to the other. Your plan is your true north and it allows you to stop and re-align along the way to ensure you are going in the right direction. There is a popular saying, "The harder I work, the luckier I get," and I firmly believe it, but at the same time it is essential that we have a plan in the first place. Remember, if you aim at nothing you will hit it every time.

Personally, one of the ways that I check that we are on track with where we are meant to be is by purposely creating planning sessions. Often I will drop the children to school and close by is a very cool organic café. As a side note, the fact they make sensational coffee, of which I choose to sample while there, is just the sacrifice I have to make for going there to plan, but I suffer through that beautiful coffee to get my planning done. Hey, someone has to do it!

This is generally about 8.20am in the morning, the time where by now my emails are really starting to go pretty crazy, my phone is ringing, and I have way more 'important' things to do than plan. People 'urgently' seem to need me, and I feel the pressure to respond promptly.

However, so often we let the seemingly urgent tasks – that

email that just popped in, the person who wants to talk right now – get in the way of checking the road map for where we are meant to be going. An 8.20am planning time is very inconvenient, but it is essential that we keep checking (sometimes daily) where we are going.

In my case, we are running multiple divisions and as such I have multiple balls to juggle. Media and advertising is constantly changing in this Digital Age and as such I literally need to keep re-correcting our position in the marketplace on what feels like a weekly basis. In your case that might be complete overkill; you might not need to look at planning anywhere near as much as I do. But do you stop and just have time out to think about your life and business and where it is going?

To do business debt-free, to come up with new ideas, to start new divisions, to swim upstream: much of these ideas and strategies will not happen while you're sitting at your desk attending to the day's business. Or for those on the go, racing from job site to job site, constantly attending to the immediate needs. This is all the additional work you do that sets you apart. Running a business is demanding and requires our active involvement and you don't need to be planning at 8.20am. That may not work for you, especially if you are in micro business and you don't get paid if you stop working. But you still need to find that time, before or after hours, to check the road map and see where you are going.

As a rugby fan, I'll read in the paper (actually, more online these days) about the player who has really stepped it up and is having a great year. When queried by the journalists as to why the player has gone to another level, it is generally because they get to training early and stay late, doing the extra work that is not actually required by the coach, but will make the difference nonetheless. They did extra sessions in the off-season, they watched their diet while the other players were 'letting their hair down' and they were planning and preparing in advance for the upcoming season.

It might also be those extra gym sessions in the week, that scheduled meeting with a nutritionist, strength coach, and so on that sees this athlete doing the 'one-percenters': all the little things that make the difference in a very competitive environment.

A good friend of mine has worked in high-level sport for most of his life – first as a player, then as a coach. A couple of years back, in late January, he had one of the biggest names in rugby league come and stay at his house for the week. When I inquired as to how on earth the coach let his star player stay away from training so close to the start of the season, my friend advised that this player was so disciplined and trained so hard away from the team that the coach had no issues with it. That would be a first at that level of sport, I would say, but his commitment and dedication to training put him in a 'league' of his own.

A place to dream
I read some years ago that Walt Disney used to have a 'dreaming' office. When he wanted to get away from the day-to-day pressures and the pull on his time to keep the operation running smoothly, he would slip into another room, free of paperwork, bills and other issues a CEO must deal with and just dream. While Walt Disney is the ultimate visionary, you don't have to be at his level to still find the space in your life to see where you need to be going.

For me it is that café, plus a few other spots where I can really dream. There's a particular room in my home, certain streets where I used to walk my dog each evening, and also a particular beach I like to walk in the early morning. The deck by my pool is also another 'dream' place for me. As you train yourself to dream and think outside the square, you too will find places you can think with clarity. It will take time to find them and to train your mind to de-clutter, but the benefits will be immeasurable.

A couple of years ago, we were back in Sydney to visit family when I took our dog for a walk one evening. My Dad, who sadly passed away in 2016, only lived a few streets away from the family home we had sold before moving to Queensland, and as such my evening walk used to go through the pathway that was not too far from where we lived. It was one of my key prayer walks and as I walked it I really connected with God along it. Interestingly, as soon as I hit that path where I used to pray each evening, it was like I had never left. Within a few minutes of walking I slipped straight into that place where my mind deletes all of the day's concerns and challenges and immediately I could get clarity and dream.

Simultaneously when we moved north, it probably took me about three months to create an evening walking track where I could achieve the same. I'd hit the streets with my trusty Labrador in tow, but it took me ages to find that groove again. I'd walk for a long time and couldn't slip into a time of prayer easily. So I encourage you to find that time and space where you can let your mind 'breathe'. It is honestly one of my secrets to success. God reveals so much to me in those quiet times. It may be just one small change that He reveals that could literally change your life. He is the world's cheapest life and business coach!

Always remember to keep your strongest ally – God – front and center and allow time to dream.

Failing to plan is planning to fail.
BENJAMIN FRANKLIN

CHAPTER THREE

THE SURF LIFESTYLE

From a young age, I apparently had a lot of energy. My parents often remarked on just how much energy I had. Like most young children, I slept in a cot until I was big enough to leave the safety of the bars behind and shift into a bed. Out of impatience, when my parents would put me down to sleep, as soon as I would wake I would use my head to head butt out each of the timber bars. I managed to remove every one of the bars out of the cot, and so was moved to a bed well before I was ready.

However, this energy didn't change a whole lot. When I would wake, instead of head butting the bars, I started head butting the wall that my bed was placed up against. Little by little I would use my head as a battering ram, until I put my head straight through the plasterboard. Luckily there wasn't a beam there or I may have caused some serious long-term brain damage… Be careful who you talk to as some people may say I did! It may explain a lot of things to those who know me…

My Dad was fairly talented with his hands and fortunately was able to fix the wall, but to this day I have never heard of a child that has done what I had. From there I could be found hitting my head on the concrete driveway. Both my parents believe it was energy and a desperation to get going that was causing this, and not anger. They recall that I was a very happy child, but was just in a hurry to get going. I was able to make full sentences by 16 months of age, and so I was obviously in a hurry to get on with it and discover life.

As a footnote, my parents have received some of their own back, as our third child Hayden, may have inherited his father's energy. We affectionately call him 'Hayden-in-a-Hurry', as he was born in the car. The energy he has and the pace he lives life at is exemplified in the fact that he just didn't have the patience to make it to the hospital to arrive. In fact, his birth certificate states that he was born at the Shell Service Station, Warringah Road, Forestville. (Sydney, Australia.)

That is a story for later, but suffice to say that being on hand to see your child being born in the passenger seat of the car – all the while having his big brother and sister strapped into their car seats just behind – is a moment we will never forget. But Hayden, like me as a child, cannot slow down until about a half an hour before he is ready for bed. Outside of this, he can literally kick the ball all day, causing my wife and I to collapse on the couch when he finally drifts off to sleep. I know he'll use all that energy for something great one day. My wife always says, "What walks in the father runs in the son." Never a truer word spoken!

A 'grommet' was born

I was 4 years of age when my parents' marriage broke down, and like any child who goes through divorce, this was not easy. At such a young age, I did not quite understand what was going on, and years later I was thankful that my parents decided to move on while my sister and I were not old enough to really comprehend the impact this would have on all of our lives. Being so young (my sister is 18 months older than me, and so was 5 or 6 years old at the time) I guess we never really knew what it was like to have Mum and Dad under the same roof, and as such I grew up feeling that this was normal (for us). Not easy, but normal.

To my parents' credit, they always got on exceptionally well and were always friends. Never once have I heard my mother or father talk poorly of the other in front of my sister or me, and that has had a lasting impact on both of our lives. Funnily enough, right to the end of my Dad's life they got on tremendously well and would catch up for a cup of tea a couple of times a week. So even at my age now, with me being a parent of four beautiful young children, the fact that my parents had a great relationship – albeit they lived separate lives – was an extremely comforting fact.

When my parents broke up, my Dad met another woman and, in the process, bought a home on the beach. When I say *on the beach*, I don't mean near the beach, but *on* it. Our backyard emptied onto the sand.

Due to where my Dad lived, my sister and I pestered my Mum to move closer to both him and the ocean. At this stage we were living about a 20 minute drive inland, so we sold up and also moved to the beachside suburb of Narrabeen. Mum's house was about a fifteen minute walk from Dad's.

While surfing is an elite sport in this day and age, the surf lifestyle has always been a fairly loose one. Alcohol and drugs were a major part of it, and surfing has always had the reputation as a sport where its partakers work as little as possible so they can enjoy maximum time in the water. Again, that perception is changing, but was certainly this way when I was growing up.

The sport is so addictive that you just want to do more of it. If you happen to be able to ride a surfboard with some level of competence, then – and only then – can you vouch for what I mean. A surfer can be lost for hours out in the water. The only sports that come close (in my mind) are skiing, snowboarding, skateboarding and waterskiing, but still, none of these really compare to a surf, as every wave is different. I have spent many years down at the snowfields, and while a week at the snow is fantastic, the mountain never changes. After a week I am happy to go home.

Learning to surf at such a young age, coupled with my proximity to the ocean, I became pretty competent early on. I entered my first surfing contest at the age of 10, which, back then was very young. Now though, as a new generation of dedicated surfers have had children and have them down the beach and on a surfboard at a very young age, a ten year-old doing contests would not be considered young.

My youngest son is now 9 and he started his surfing contests at 6, so he has had a four year head start on me. For me though, my Dad was an ex-rugby player, and although he lived on the beach, he was far from comfortable in the ocean. In fact, he bought a surf ski (that we affectionately named the 'goat boat') so that he could enjoy the waves with us. Watching him paddling out and trying to catch waves, all the while having the surf ski's seat belt buckled around his waist, literally brought me to a panic. He always seemed to time his paddle 'out the back' just as the sets (the bigger waves) were starting to loom. He'd simply spent a lifetime away from the ocean, even though he lived his life on the Northern Beaches of Sydney. As a man in his 40's, trying to understand the ocean, all the while buckled in on that ski, was really a recipe for disaster. He did actually hurt himself pretty badly on a few occasions.

North Narrabeen

Dad's house was at South Narrabeen, about a one mile distance from the infamous waves of North Narrabeen. That's where the serious surfers plied their trade, and a few world champions have come from this surfing powerhouse. At the time I was growing up, the local legend was Damien Hardman, who went on to win the 1987 and 1991 world titles. So having a world champion at your local beach break is a pretty big deal. This was back in the days when the Northern Beaches was home to most of Australia's professional surfers. Now, they are all mostly based in Queensland and northern New South Wales, where the water is warmer and the waves are better. North Narrabeen has always been a tough beach, and still is to this day. In fact, only a few short years ago, a local guy was put in prison for intimidating people whilst out in the surf. He would chase guys out of the water, knock fins out of their surfboards with his bare hands, and generally use his large frame to frighten the life out of all who encountered him. And boy did it work!

To this day, many surfers will cruise along the northern coastline of Sydney, keen to find the best waves. They will stop and check North Narrabeen, but very few will actually paddle out. The reputation this place still has means the locals get the waves mostly to themselves. Only the very brave – or very competent – dare venture out.

'Surfie'

By about the age of 12 the local newspaper, *The Manly Daily*, chose to run a feature on some of the top 'grommets' (a grommet being a junior surfer) in the area. Given there are some 13 beaches between Manly to the south and Palm Beach to the north, to be chosen as one of the up-and-coming surfers was a pretty major compliment. I still remember going to school the day the article was published featuring me. Each week they would feature one selected surfer, and this day was my turn.

As I arrived at school I could see the looks I was getting. Clearly many people had read *The Manly Daily* that morning while eating their cereal. Remember, this was well before the Internet, when you had to read your news in print. I was very proud of this, as I was still in Grade 6, which is one year off high school. So to do this in my primary school years was something that made me feel very special.

Back in my day, most of the kids who lived near the beach surfed. There was not the range of sports that there are now. There were no real computer games, except for Space Invaders, Donkey Kong and Pacman, and so you'd get home from school, and other than homework, which wasn't very appealing, you could hit the waves. I went to a school in the suburb of Terrey Hills. Terrey Hills is probably only 15-20 minutes' drive from the beach, and in terms of how big Sydney is, it really is still classified as a suburb of the Northern Beaches. But to a guy like me, who lived on the beach, it may as well have been on the other side of Sydney. How dare my parents send me so far inland to do my schooling when all of my mates at the beach went to the local public schools nearby!

My parents decided to send my sister and I to a school called Northern Beaches Christian School. That was very uncool of them, or so I thought at the time. Known as NBCS, it was a very strict school, and very strong on appearance. Whether it was 38 degrees (100 in Farenheit) or higher, our shirts had to be tucked in, our socks pulled up to just under the knee, and top button secured, with your tie covering it. No exceptions. School shoes were inspected daily by the prefects in the morning at assembly to ensure that they were well polished. So for a guy from the beach, where the surf lifestyle is a relaxed one, I had this other world where I had to be very disciplined.

As Terrey Hills was not on the beach, a large majority of the attendees were from the North Shore of Sydney. While today the Northern Beaches is more expensive to buy property in than the North Shore, that was not the case back in my day. With a closer proximity to the city, the North Shore was the place to be. St Ives was the top suburb, and a high proportion of our students resided there. So while those kids loved the ocean, they were not brought up as the ocean dwellers as we who lived right on the coast were.

To put into perspective how insular our lives were in living by the beach, my stepbrother used to proudly tell people that, "Anyone who lives on the other side of Pittwater Road is a westie." Pittwater Road was the street that our house was on, and so effectively what he was saying was that if you lived across the road (from the beach, I might add), then you were a 'westie'. And in case you're not aware, 'westie' is derived from Sydney's western suburbs, which are far from the coast. So being called a westie is not a compliment! Westies take trains and buses to get to the beach as they live so far from it.

Accordingly, with a (mostly) non-surfing school population, my nickname very quickly became 'Surfie'. My hair was bleached blonde from the sun and I happened to appear in the newspaper a few more times. Hence the name. I didn't mind, as it brought a bit of notoriety, and it also kept me in good stead with some of the older, tougher kids. I was well liked at school and so didn't ever have to go to school dreading being bullied, as many do.

At this stage of my life my dream was to become a professional surfer. My mother hated the idea, as she had much higher hopes for me than being a guy who spent his life at the beach. I continued entering surfing competitions and getting good results, and at a young age I really felt that becoming a professional surfer was achievable if I was to keep heading in that direction. I was competitive with a few guys who went on to make that elusive World Tour, so the opportunity was at least there.

Interestingly, one afternoon my Mum went for a walk on the beach, as she loved to do, and ended up right in the corner of North Narrabeen, where she saw Damien Hardman in action. With Damien being the world's top surfer of that time, watching him ride waves was like watching an incredible artist paint a blank canvas. You could watch him for hours, just in sheer disbelief that someone had that much creativity – let alone skill – on that moving wave. I still remember that day changing Mum's world in that she now had a newfound respect for surfing at an elite level. It really is one of the hardest sports to master and those that are competent have very high skill levels.

My first sponsorship

At the age of 12 I struck up a friendship with a great Christian guy called Wayne Ryan. Wayne was heavily involved in a global ministry called 'Christian Surfers' and thought I should meet a friend of his who had his own surfboard business. Phil Nichol was his name, and he owned a surfboard company aptly named 'Nichol'. Nichol agreed to sponsor me and so I was getting free surfboards from the age of 12. This was all thanks to Wayne.

However, I learnt the business lesson of not burning your bridges at a very young age. To be that age and receiving brand new surfboards free of charge was a very big honor, especially since the surfing industry was still somewhat in its developmental years. But respecting people in business was something I was yet to learn. About a year into my Nichol sponsorship, I was surfing at a particular part of Narrabeen when I noticed there was someone watching me. Now in this day and age, if I told my parents that some guy was watching me in the surf, they wouldn't let me out of their sight for fear that the man may have had some ulterior motive.

I used to imagine this guy was from a major surfing corporation and that he was watching me for sponsorship purposes. So while I was surfing I would push my manouvers to the limit to really show off my skills. It turns out that he *was* from the surf industry, but not in such a major way. A friend from the beach said that he was the owner of the Power Linez Surf Shop in Narrabeen. His name was Roger and he wanted to meet me. A middle-aged guy with a thick South African accent, Roger proceeded to inform me that he, through a major surfboard brand, 'Town & Country', wanted to sign me to ride their boards.

While I was happy to ride for Nichol, Nichol, to put it in perspective, was a small brand from Wollongong, about an hour south of Sydney. Town & Country, on the other hand, was a global one, birthed out of Hawaii, the surfing mecca. To paint the picture for the non-surfer, this would be similar to a model being signed to *GAP* clothing when *Ralph Lauren* comes calling. Or a celebrity signing with *Avon* when *Chanel* is also waving a contract around. It is simply several levels up.

I happily accepted the new sponsorship, which took my credibility at the beach to a new level. Free boards from Nichol was pretty cool, but free boards from Town & Country was on a whole new level. Today, Town & Country, tomorrow Quiksilver, was the way I was thinking. While I was only young, the way I handled the Nichol affair was not right. I never called Nichol to explain and instead only casually mentioned to Wayne that I'd no longer be riding for Nichol, as Town & Country had offered me a deal. Wayne never said much and I handed him back my current Nichol board when my new Town & Country arrived. Luckily in those days everyone was a little more relaxed, so it was no big deal.

However, while I was feeling pretty proud of myself, the deal with Town & Country never seemed to go anywhere. I got my first free board from them, but my contact, Roger, soon after sold his shop and so was nowhere to be found when I needed another board. I had no contact at Town & Country, as my dealings were all through him, and so, tail between my legs, I went to Wayne stating I'd be more than happy to ride for Nichol again. Surprisingly, Nichol simply picked up where we left off, supplying me with a new board at no cost.

It was a lesson I learned at an age when most have not yet come across this sort of situation. That lesson is: don't burn your bridges. It worked out okay for me this time, but I couldn't go on treating people like this and expect to have fruitful relationships. Business has to be win-win, and as soon as you get this out of balance, there is going to be a breakdown at some point in each and every business relationship or agreement.

The passion changed

As I progressed to my teenage years, I found myself becoming less interested in being a pro surfer and more interested in the business side of things. I had no idea what was driving this, but for some strange reason this is where I started to see a different passion. As I would turn up to the contests I had entered, which sometimes was three and four in a month, I started to develop a keen interest in the different surfboard brands. I'd do the same when I went into the surf shops also. I started getting fascinated by the different wetsuit and clothing companies, which, at the time, were still run by surfers who would stop working if the swell was up. They were on their way to creating billion-dollar enterprises, but they didn't realize this. They still had a long way to go, but they were doing what they loved and enjoying the journey, and that was all that mattered.

I look at the surfing industry now and it is a multi-billion dollar global industry. Many of the surfers who started those companies are long gone, replaced by private equity, publicly listed corporations, and acquisitions by big leisure brands who have come in and gobbled up the surfing industry. So it has also been interesting watching that industry go from one where the guys in it got there because of their love and passion for surfing, and not just their desire to make money. (As a sidenote for anyone interested there is a great book detailing the surf industry's movement from surfers owning the companies to the corporates taking over. It's called *Salts & Suits* and is written by a great surf journalist from my area of Noosa, Phil Jarratt.)

That left a lasting impression on me. I learned some great lessons growing up and watching surfing go from a Mum-and-Dad style of operation to the global corporations of today.

They key lesson is this: **don't just do things for money**! In a world where there are so many ways in which you can make money, aim to make it through something you are passionate about. It takes every ounce of your energy, determination and sacrifice to build a career and make money, so if you are not passionate about your industry or job, then you will burn out very quickly.

People are always intrigued about why top business people, sports stars or entertainers can keep going, even though they may have millions of dollars in the bank. How does that top sports person continue to travel the globe, having to be ruthless about his/her preparation, diet, sleep and so on, not to mention the pressure they are under, when they could be seeing the best sights, eating the best food and drinking the best wine as they fly around the world? What is it that drives them on long after they are financially secure? While to a degree they would enjoy the money and the power (potentially also the fame, more in the case of the sports person than the business person) that accompanies their success, at the same time they have a deep-found passion for what they do. They got there because of that passion and they can continue to remain there because of it also.

This is exactly the point where my desire for being a pro-surfer faded. I didn't have the relaxed personality for performing well in surf contests. As I got older I would get so nervous to perform in those twenty minute heats that I started to 'freeze' up, performing poorly. I was starting to get beaten by guys who I should have been beating, and so while my love for surfing did not die, my love of contests surely did. It takes a certain personality type that can remain calm between heats, often sitting around for hours – sometimes days - when they may only be surfing four to five times, with 20 minutes of competition time at a go. It just didn't suit my go-for-broke personality with its stop-start nature. I was starting to get passionate about another area in my life, and surfing contests was not going to be part of my future.

Power Surfboards

Such was my interest in business that I was starting to generate, a friend of mine and I decided to start our own surfboard company. We called it 'Power Surfboards' and while we never went to the trouble of registering the business name, we had a great time developing a logo that would sit under the fiber-glassed boards. I still remember sitting in class designing logos for 'Power' while the teacher talked. My mind was elsewhere, dreaming and scheming. I knew how much it cost to make a surfboard, I knew how much we could sell them for, and if I was not at school, but rather making and selling boards each week, then it would be pretty easy to carve out a living.

Together my friend Josh and I went halves in a foam blank so that we could make our first board. We built a small surfboard factory down the side of my Mum's house, complete with fitting a roof and door. Josh happened to know a local surfboard builder and he let us into his factory to show us how surfboards were made. From there we created a full factory so we could start our business. We had big plans so we thought we better build our surfboard factory before starting the business. Josh and I built the surfboard racks that hold that foam blank so that when the blank is sitting flat on the racks, or sitting in the 'v' section so you could work on the sides – otherwise known as the rails – we had the racks that the professionals used. We bought steel bins, we created the v-shaped racks, and then we bought and mixed up cement so we could secure the racks in the bins. With the factory built and the racks in the middle of it, we were ready to go.

Together we made a surfboard that had our name on it. It was a massive process, but by the time it was completed, it was ride-able. Just. Did I mention it was ugly, horrible and that we would have had to pay someone to take it off our hands? That was beside the point. We had our first board completed. The main issue we struck was that, while Josh was quite good with his hands, I was not. I was – and still am – terrible. So while I had visions of running the company side of things, we weren't big enough for that yet. We needed two guys who could both use their hands to make boards if we were to properly launch this, but instead we only had one. And as creating surfboards is a time-consuming job, having one guy do all the work was never going to fit our small company.

So while we decided to stop making boards, from that young age I learnt the skill of setting up a business. I just seemed to know how to get an idea, run with it, and then see it materialize into a venture that could make money. Josh and I weren't driven by money, but rather passion, so while we stopped after that first board, in our eyes, we were a success. We had done exactly what we had set out to do. We were kids, we were having fun and that was what we were really after. Money was not the end goal.

Even to this day I don't over-think any aspect of business. Again, business is supply and demand, and if there is the demand, then it is your job to figure out how to create the supply. Guys are buying surfboards every day of the year, so by creating a brand – and then hopefully good surfboards – it really could have been quite easy to capitalize on this. But while this is a feel-good story, there could easily have been a very dark lining to the silver cloud. Surfboards are made from carved foam. Easy, straight forward and not dangerous. Once the style is shaped into the foam with a planer, you then roll a layer of fiberglass over the foam blank. From there you mix up resin, which is highly flammable, and this is poured over the fiberglass layer, causing the resin to set, and in the process creating that hard, waterproof finish. (Sounds pretty easy, hey?) So it's a highly flammable process.

Honestly, we could have burnt the house down at any moment. We were doing this work in a completely uncontrolled environment and with a timber fence one side and gardens all around us, not a lot would need to go wrong before we could have had a serious issue on our hands. Also, because the surfboard was over six feet in length, we needed a lot of resin to complete the board. This was highly dangerous stuff. I still remember finishing the first coat of resin and while it was drying, Josh and I went to the local store to buy a milkshake. I distinctly recall smelling that resin about a block from my home as it was drying. Now I realize why surfboards must be made in factories, which can only be built in areas zoned for 'industrial'…

God was certainly watching over us. Had the house burned down, or God forbid, the neighbor's place, I'm certain Mum's insurance would not have covered it.

Giving up is the ultimate tragedy.
ROBERT J. DONOVAN

CHAPTER FOUR

GRANDMA'S GENES

My grandmother was a woman well before her time. Sadly she died in her 50s, while I was probably only about 8 years-old, and even worse is that the illness she had would have easily been managed with today's modern medicine. So I really didn't get to know her all that well – given my young age and how hard she worked.

Nevertheless, 'Nanna Betty', as we called her – short for Elizabeth – was a phenomenal woman. In an era where Australian women stayed at home and looked after the children, she was out doing business deals. Buying property and developing it before on-selling it was her forte, or she would put tenants in her properties and enjoy the weekly rent. I remember as a young boy getting on the Manly ferry – at the Manly, not the city end – and looking at the different houses along Sydney Harbour that Nanna owned. I distinctly remember being on the southern side of the ferry, on the way to the city, with my mother and sister calling out 'That's

Nanna's house;" 'That's Nanna's house." In today's money those three properties would probably be around $8-10 million each (not in total). One of the grandest memories I have of my Nanna was the bright yellow Porsche she used to drive around. As young kids, having a grandmother with such a fancy sports car was basically unheard of, but she was far from your average woman, let alone grandmother. I also remember that every time she opened her handbag, she had wads of cash. Cash just seemed to be everywhere...

If she was traveling overseas, her return was such an exciting event, as she literally bought us bags of presents. While she was a driven lady and very hard on my Mum, she absolutely loved her grandkids. But oddly she hated the colour green. There could be no green anywhere near her. Luckily she was not born in America, where all the money is green, and to this day I don't know what the driver was of this superstition.

My Nanna's drive probably resulted in the breakdown of her marriage. My 'Pop', as we called him, was one of nature's true gentlemen. A carpet salesman by day, his true loves were swimming and surf lifesaving, and in later life, bowls. You would be hard pressed to find a nicer guy than my Pop, and as such, the differences in personality just drove them apart. He had the time of day for anyone and was loved by all. He worked to live, whereas his wife was the polar opposite.

Nanna was moving from just property purchasing and holdings into property development when she was approached by a young man keen to get into the same game. Harry Triguboff was his name. To those who live outside of Australia, the name Harry Triguboff would mean nothing to them. But Harry has been right near the top of Australia's rich list, the BRW Rich 200 (Australia's version of the *Forbes Rich List*) for some decades as the sole owner of Meriton.

Even to this day, a quick scan of the list sees Harry (as I type this in 2018) is listed as Australia's richest person, with an estimated wealth of $12.77 billion.[1]

Together, I believe, they developed a block of units in the Sydney suburb of Gladesville. I don't think their relationship went any further than that one development, but it was the birthing of the business career of one of Australia's most successful and prominent businessmen. As I write this book, I saw Harry interviewed on television for an English documentary looking at Australia today when he said he believed that some five to six percent of Sydney's population currently live in one of his properties.

Meriton has gone on to be an absolute success, and even though Harry is now 85 years-old, his business cannot slow down. Back to business being about supply and demand, the New South Wales Government, the government that controls the city of Sydney, has made a directive that Sydney cannot spread any further out. The sprawl has gone as far as it can and as such the entire city (not just the downtown area) needs to go up.

As Meriton specializes in building massive blocks of units, Sydney's move to high rise means his business is laughing all the way to the bank. And as Sydney pushes towards being a city of ten million people in the next decade or so, a quick calculation shows that if five percent of its current population of 5 million live in Meriton apartments, then that is some 250,000 people

---

1 https://www.afr.com/brand/afr-magazine/rich-list-overview-20180413-h0yqo5

that Harry has done business with. And not selling them a $4.00 cup of coffee, but more likely a half a million dollar property. Supply and demand.

The Jewish connection

About five years ago, my mother decided to make contact with Harry. She tracked him down via his offices and managed to set up a time to meet with him. She simply called his personal assistant, explained who she was, and when the message got to him, he invited her to meet with him. I spoke to her the day that they met and asked her how the meeting went and her response was: "He was actually very cranky and seemed really busy." Plus he did say to her, "You're not like your mother at all," in reference to the fact that my mother inherited her father's, not her mother's, temperament.

At the end of the meeting, she caught the lift to the ground floor in Sydney's downtown, where his offices are based, where a newsstand happened to be located. She bought a copy of *The Australian Financial Review*, which is *The Wall Street Journal* of Australia, where that day's front page news was 'Harry Triguboff's $450m fight with the ATO' (Australian Tax Office). I remember talking to my Mum on the phone saying, "Mum, you cannot even imagine what it must be like living in a world like his. Sure, he has riches that we cannot begin to imagine, but the stress of running a company of that size means he operates on a level of pressure and stress that few could ever bear."

Literally running a multi-billion dollar company with thousands of staff, and in one of the toughest industries there is – high-rise property development – would have pressures that would cause the average person to have a nervous breakdown, several times over. But the fact that Nanna was there at the start of one of the world's most successful businessmans career was a pretty big deal. At the time of writing this, he had rejected an offer to sell his private company for a multi-billion dollar sum. Now in his 80s, he still works out with his trainer every morning before driving straight to the office. Because of supply and demand, business has never been better, and with the changes happening in Sydney, Meriton might just be about to enter its golden era. Everything it has done to date may just be a warm up for what is to come. And he still hasn't entered the other major cities of Australia...

In conclusion

Nanna-Betty had adopted a *NOT Business As Usual* way of doing things. Her age, the era she lived in and the fact that other women her age were 'keeping house' and raising children made her unique. In many ways I see myself in my Nanna. Her passion, her drive, her determination, coupled with her love of business, and I see that I definitely inherited 'Grandma's Genes'.

I use not only all the brains I have but all I can borrow.
WOODROW WILSON

CHAPTER FIVE

COMPOUNDING INTEREST

My first serious job was as a milkman. I must be showing my age, as the business of home delivering milk to people is long gone. I worked two afternoons one week and three the next. One week I earned $16, the next $24, and on it went. While most boys my age (I was 12 years-old at the time) probably would have wanted to spend their earnings, I enjoyed nothing more than saving it. I remember going to the bank every month or so with wads of cash, and I just loved watching the number grow in my bankbook.

The teller would take my cash deposit, and the balance on my deposit book would print out the new, higher figure when they handed it back to me. To me, that was fascinating. Watching those numbers grow from my hard work was really satisfying. I lost my love for drinking milk, as I was now constantly smelling the off milk that had been spilt in the van, but other than that, seeing the fruit – or the milk – of my labor made all the hard work worthwhile.

The other thing that really got my attention was the word

'interest', which also accrued as I deposited more cash. I learned an interesting lesson at a young age: if you don't spend all your money, then you are not only saving money, but you're earning money on the money invested by way of interest. 'Compounding interest' is what they call it, and it grows the more you save.

I have never been money hungry, even at that young age, but I just enjoyed knowing that as I was earning money, it was continuing to increase. My lifestyle was incredibly simple. Surfing was free, and so there was really nothing I needed. Other than a milkshake and a (very) regular bag of jellies to satisfy my incredibly sweet tooth, I have always enjoyed the very simple things in life. To this day I have learned to live without a lot. I love nice things, as we all do, but I am not governed by them. I'll choose the steak over the sausages any day of the week, and there have been many seasons in business where life has been about sausages, not steak. But in life I have learnt to be content either way. I love Paul's words in Philippians 4:11-12:

I am not saying this because I am in need, for I have learned to be content whatever the circumstances. I know what it is to be in need, and I know what it is to have plenty. I have learned the secret of being content in any and every situation, whether well fed or hungry, whether living in plenty or in want."

Ever the entrepreneur

Another successful way of producing income that I found was from selling my surf contest prizes to friends. Being a junior surfer, there was no prize money anywhere to be found. In fact prize money does not start until you are in the professional ranks. It's all for love! If you received a placing in the finals of the event, then your 'winnings' were a trophy and prizes. All the surf companies would provide the prizes, as they sponsored the events, and so it was normal to walk away from an event with backpacks, towels, hats, wetsuits, and the like.

While the surf industry has met a lot more competition in the last few years – and especially since the Global Financial Crisis – in those days everyone was desperate for a Billabong backpack, a Rip Curl towel, or a Quiksilver wallet. Anything with one of the surf labels on it was highly sought after. Did I mention they were expensive? All the kids *had* to wear surf clothes, even if they couldn't stand on a surfboard, so these prizes, when sold at a slight discount, went pretty quickly. Living on the beach meant we had a way bigger network of people to sell to than the average family did. Plus many of the kids from my school who lived on the North Shore wanted to look like they surfed, so these must-have accessories helped them look like they were part of the surfing fraternity.

In fact, the surfing industry was starting to grow so quickly that a local guy who owned a surf shop in Collaroy, one suburb south of where I lived, opened a store in Penrith. If you're a 'westie' in Sydney, then you're an 'ultra-westie' if you lived in Penrith. At the foot of the Blue Mountains, it was a 90 minute drive to the beach, yet surf gear was massively popular, even out there.

By the time I finished school I had $17,000 in the bank. I'd barely spent a cent, saved all my money, saw my interest compound, and also learnt that the simple things in life were by far the best. As I've aged, I have found this not always to be the case. I'm now a lover of beautiful foods, I like fine wines, and I have a taste for expensive clothing. Life does get more complicated as we get older, but to this day, I choose to live my life as Paul suggested in Corinthians: to be satisfied with little, or to be satisfied with much.

Once you can control your spending and desires, buying things when you can truly afford them, then you've found one of the secrets to a simple, happy life. To this day I try and find things that don't cost a lot of money to enjoy. From a swim at the beach, to a coffee at a local café whilst reading the newspaper, to swimming in our pool, or sitting on the deck to read and write, we find things that we enjoy, but also don't mean we are constantly consuming. It also sets an example for our kids to not lead consumer-driven lives.

My wife and I try and live our lives this way. Okay, more me than my wife. She loves to shop! We carry no credit cards, even though this means we lose a lot of rewards points, but it means that we cannot buy things on a day-to-day basis unless we have cash in the bank. It also means we have to control our expenses, as we don't live in a buy-now-pay-later world. We do have one credit card that we use to pay business bills, but only in the case where we need to pay a bill that is due and payable before we have the cash, but generally speaking this really controls our expenses. Neither our business or personal lives are run by credit. Plus it helps me to sleep soundly at night, especially as I have the added responsibility of my wife and I being employed by our company, along with others we are responsible for. While we're at the stage of life where we are not saving a ton of money – three children in private school (and one to go through soon) and the associated expenses cleans you out pretty quickly – we simply cannot live beyond our means.

I often say to my wife that even if we had a billion dollars in the bank, our lives would not look that different. I have found that the truly simple things are what really do make me happy.

Sure, we might eat Scotch Fillet more often and go for salmon steaks over chops. We'd probably eat out more. But otherwise, we are content with what we have. We are always striving for more, as our business is our ministry, but we are 'striving' not just to make more money, but to do something really worthwhile with our lives for the Kingdom of God. Our children are watching on and seeing how we operate, and so not only do we desire to leave a legacy, but to also set an example for them that they need to strive for something greater than just themselves. And greater than just money and accumulating 'stuff'. Money comes with being good at what you do, so there's no need to chase it.

Life is not just about paying your bills and looking out for you; life is about doing something great, something worthwhile, and using the talents that God has freely given you. I have found that the money always takes care of itself. There is simply no need to chase it.

A different financial model
When you're a business owner, you need to live on a different financial path to those who are employed. Sure, you can make a lot more money than those on a fixed wage, but with this comes the stress and strain of balancing cash flow as you wait for jobs to sgn off, people to pay you, and so on. I think cash flow is one of the hardest parts in managing a debt-free business, or any business, for that matter. Staff payments come first. Our team have always been paid before we are, so you need to come up with a different way of managing your personal finances if you have a business that might constantly be waiting on payments from clients. That is the case with our business. Being in media, our clients buy advertising and creative services, retailers and distributors order

books, authors are flying all over the world, and we are getting their stock to speaking venues in advance for them, and so our services and stock are generally released before we are paid. And because this puts a strain on our cash flow, it also means that we need to operate on a different financial platform to the husband and wife who might both work for other people, or where one is self employed and the other has the steady job.

Hard lessons to learn

I remember having coffee with a guy some years ago who had been very successful in his career with a Fortune 500 company. He had a large salary as a manager in this large firm before deciding to strike out on his own. At the time of leaving his stable employment to start his business, he had a few properties, each one secured against the other. He also had a very big mortgage on his primary residence. This risky investment model was fine for a guy who had that large income inside the security of a big company, but as he left that world and struck out on his own, he had not adjusted his personal financial world to suit his new position. Like everyone starting out in business, it was slower to take off than his business plan no doubt anticipated, and before long it all went pear-shaped.

By the time we met for a coffee it was all over for him. The banks had called in the loans and it was the beginning of the end, but I remember advising that as a business owner you simply cannot take the investment risks that those stably employed can. Many do, and all is fine while the payments are being made, but it doesn't take a lot to go wrong before it all starts to cave in. While there was not a happy ending in all of this for my colleague, I can report that he and his family have clawed their way back, started from scratch and made amends. They have built a new home and are recovering well financially. However I am sure the emotional turmoil is the thing that would still cause the pain. There would be an emotional scar there that would take a long time to heal, if ever.

Even at the top end of the corporate world, there was the story where Rupert Murdoch's entire media empire nearly collapsed under the weight of one small bank in middle-America. Murdoch's company, News Corporation (which is now split in two: the print assets are under News Corporation still, but the TV and entertainment assets are under a new entity, 21st Century Fox, which has just been sold to Disney) had hundreds of millions of dollars in loans, but a small bank wanted its small loan back, which nearly brought the entire company undone. It had taken on too much debt to buy TV stations and the Fox film group in the US. News negotiated with its banks, sold assets and survived. But if it can happen to Rupert Murdoch, then it can happen to you and me.

A life without regret

There is always the ability to come back though. Never doubt that. Plus there are a multitude of books out there that will help you mount your comeback. However, I always try and live my life along the lines that I don't want to have to come back. How can I live with wisdom today so that I make the right decisions, which will mean I am not always on the comeback trail?

That entrepreneurial path of making it big, losing it all, making it big again, losing it all again… Some people wear this like it is a badge of honor, but it personally doesn't appeal to me. What people fail to realize is the emotional scars that this places on your life. You can always make your comeback, but you don't want to make it a habit, as it will take a massive toll on your life, and potentially your marriage, children and the like. I have enough business scars and bruises to last a lifetime and I have never been bankrupted.

Even in the church world we can accidentally over-celebrate those who have had rough lives, then made their redemption. It's understandable, as it can be a great way to get people in the church's doors. From the ex-con who met God, to the ex-drug addict, ex-bankrupt, ex-homeless person, and so on. They are awesome stories and testimonies of God at work, but seriously, do you want that for your life? The pain, the regret, the memories and scars... I want to be the person who doesn't have that crazy testimony because I followed God's ways. It's a daily fight to keep God and His wisdom up front and central in your life, but it's also well worth it. To those who have this style of testimony, more power to you for making it back!

Sure, we will all have some ups and downs, but I am referring here to not having to keep coming back from the jaws of business 'death'. With wise living and living within our means, we might not need to have to keep making major comebacks. "Let's do that all over again," said Nobody. Ever. Yet they do, by not learning from it and then changing their actions.

(Please note that I am not belittling or talking down to anyone who has been in this situation. I have only just escaped with my life on many occasions in business, so many of my comments are based on my own heartache and pain.)

For me, *NOT Business As Usual* is business debt-free. The banks have no involvement in our business.

Our real blessings often appear to us in the shape of pains, losses and disappointments; but let us have patience, and we soon shall see them in their proper figures.
JOSEPH ADDINGTON

CHAPTER SIX

FIRST ATTEMPTS

My business dream was always to be a publisher. From a young age, I was fascinated with the way media works. Media in Australia was also the country's highest profile area of business. Kerry Packer was on one side, and Rupert Murdoch was on the other. It made for fascinating reading – and viewing - and even those not interested in business wanted to read about what these two were up to. Their competitiveness was like watching sport. Even the non-business people were interested in them.

The Packers and Murdochs were by far the two most well known business families in Australia and so media and publishing was at the top of the tree. The only real difference between these two men was that Kerry Packer was content to contain his business interests largely within Australia, whereas Rupert was keen to expand overseas. So while they fought a battle royale within Australia, Rupert ultimately dwarfed Kerry Packer due to the businesses he acquired in other markets.

But it was not the media attention on them that drew me in. It might have helped, but at the same time I felt that there was a certain 'magic' about publishing that was completely intriguing. It interested me like nothing else did. It was as though God may have even put me on earth to be in the media business. I was too young to explain what the interest was, but God certainly knew.

However, media was to be some way off. That was not a business for an 18 year-old surfer, but rather for someone with a lot more experience than I had.

Class Grass

The day after my final high school exams were complete, I was ready to make my mark on the business world. I remember driving out west with my Dad to look at a particular vehicle. We bought a utility truck for $1500 on the spot. I bought a lawnmower, and a great Christian guy who lived down the road, Joel A'Bell, who also happened to be a great surfer, and I got started. From memory I think Joel provided the whipper-snipper to do the edging, and so we were ready to go.

Joel and I had a plan: rather than just put flyers in peoples' letterboxes, where they get thrown away, we knocked on doors. 'Class Grass' was the name of our business and we would drive the streets, park the car, and go and chase down business. Joel would take one side of the street and I the other, and we would knock on doors. We would personally introduce ourselves and hand the person our flyer, letting them know we had a new business and were eager to work. Our model worked.

My Mum was manning the phone back home, and within a week or two we had enough customers to be earning a nice amount of money, with time to fit in a lot of surfing. The success was in the fact that our potential clients got to see Joel and I face to face. Looking back, if two enterprising young guys had the courage to be able to knock on my door and personally introduce themselves, as opposed to just putting a flyer in the mail, then I would be a lot more interested in hiring them. Cold calling is not easy, and I learnt that at a young age. **Winning new business is hard, so look after the clients you have so you're not always stressing for more.**

Joel was working in the city, so he automatically picked up three hours in his day that he didn't have to sit on a bus. We have both well and truly moved on from Class Grass, both going on to bigger and better things. Joel is now one of the lead pastors at Hillsong Church, where he also works with his wife Julia. The two of them work very closely with Brian and Bobbie Houston, with Joel I believe heading up Hillsong Australia. Joel was madly in love with Julia at the time of us starting Class Grass, however Julia was from Wollongong, the same regional city where Nichol Surfboards was based, so not too long after we got started, Joel moved to Wollongong to pursue the love of his life.

Class Grass gave me a year to enjoy being out of school, but with an income stream in place so that I could find out what I wanted to do for the rest of my life. It's called a 'gap' year now, but back then, taking a year off to figure out the next step of your life was frowned upon. In many peoples' eyes, I was simply wasting a year. My parents supported me, however, and that was all that mattered to me. University was a future option, but I felt that the more practical business I did, the quicker I would get better at it. I made the decision to back myself.

Just back on Joel for a moment: it is really worth honoring him. Joel was a very good surfer who lived close to the main North

Narrabeen break. In fact just across the road. He was probably the proudest Christian surfer I knew. Many were proud when in church, but quiet when they left the church walls and entered the outside world. Not Joel. Everyone at North Narrabeen knew he was a committed Christian and at a beach that, to this day, has a worldwide reputation for producing gruff, tough surfers, this was not an easy environment to stay true to your convictions. But Joel did and he was never offended or perturbed when someone gave him a hard time. It might have helped that he was such a good surfer that he had the utmost respect of all the locals, but aside from this, Joel knew the right way to live and didn't care if someone thought he was crazy.

He left for Wollongong long before he was able to stay around and help any of these guys at any real depth on a personal level, but I have no doubt that had Joel not moved away, he would have had a massive impact on the North Narrabeen surf scene. So to see him move to Hillsong and then to the level he is at today is absolutely no surprise to me. You cannot have that strong a conviction in your personal life and not see God use you in great ways. As Matthew 9: 37 says,

"The harvest is plentiful, but the workers are few."

And in closing, this is a glimpse into God's world and the way it works. Recently in Australia, the harshness of the media spotlight on Hillsong, with Brian and Bobbie the targets, is simply a total disdain for the way God's kingdom works. These guys all started from exceptionally humble beginnings, but had a goal to build the church. They have achieved it, and rather than the world being able to celebrate their success, as they would with any other individual or organization that has worked hard and achieved their goals, they go looking for the sinister in it all.

Surely Hillsong must be just trying to 'trick' people? No, not at all. The Word of God stands, people connect with God, and the church grows. The world cannot understand it, cannot stand it, and so has to treat those in ministry like they are money hungry and in it with ulterior motives. But then they up it a step and bring in the point that they are not-for-profit and therefore are not paying tax on their profits. However, the government sets up the laws of the land, not the churches, and as such how is it the church's fault if they are not subject to tax?

In all of this, no other denomination is discussed. The Catholic Church, the Anglican Church, and so on, accept no such criticism, yet it is mostly all reserved for Hillsong. And in case you're wondering, no, I do not attend a Hillsong church and thus am not trying to defend them. I guess my point is that if you're going to step out and do something for God, there is going to be persecution. Probably a better word than persecution in our western world is 'criticism'. When I think of persecution I think of someone being stoned, beaten or imprisoned, but in our day and age, at least in the west, it is criticism, as well as cynicism.

If you're strong enough to stand up in what you believe for and you can ignore any criticism that might come your way, then God might just be able to roll out a really special plan in your life. Let me finish by saying that God will bless His people, so if you're in His will, doing His work, *expect* His blessings. Who cares if others don't understand?

Not very handy

I learnt one thing clearly in that year: I was not called to work with my hands. Not only was I not that good with them to start with, but every time I sat at my desk to do paperwork, it was like I found my home. I should have learnt that back with the surfboard 'business'. My brain was an asset but my hands were a liability. So from there it was time to work out a business model that would allow me to use my business skills, but at the same time get away from working outdoors. One thing was sure, and that was that if I was going to make my mark, it was going to have to be my brain, not my hands, that would do most of the work!

Around this time I had started doing triathlons. Triathlons were the exact opposite to surfing competitions. The gun went off, you went 'hell for leather' the entire race, then you packed up and went home. This really suited my personality and while I loved doing them, I had left my run too late. At my age, I had not spent enough years swimming, riding and running to be able to compete at the top level. I put a lot of time into training though and even entered some of the events in the pro/elite division, but by that time I just knew I was going to have to do a huge amount of work, but really could never get to the absolute top, as time was not on my side.

I had begun to do my swim training at Manly Swim Centre and as I started to scale back my lawn mowing business to just a handful of clients, the head coach was looking for someone to be his assistant coach. As it was only late afternoons and early mornings, leaving me free to do what I wanted in my days, I accepted his offer and duly became his assistant. Swimming and triathlon were completely different to surfing and I craved the change in lifestyle. This life was all about discipline. While surfing was all fun, these sports were absolutely hard work. Being a disciplined person, I loved the additional focus.

It put me in touch with a lot of people in the fitness and multi-sport industry, which was beginning to open doors without me even knowing it at the time. As an aside, I went on to coach some great young swimmers, a few who made it to the Olympics, but not all in swimming. A couple were in swimming, but then there was one in kayking and I think two in waterpolo. I was not at the swim centre for long, as I had bigger fish to fry, but it was a fantastic time of my life that also showed me a world outside of surfing.

The winning edge
I have always been a major observer and I learn a lot just by observing other people, places and organizations. For example I could observe a triathlon; how all the different components of the event come together, and then work out how to go into business based on what I had seen. I used to enjoy seeing what got into the minds of the better swimmers. At that squad we had swimmers, triathletes and surf ironmen, and working closely with them, especially the elite athletes among them, taught me so much.

But I come back to passion. This is the basic driver of all achievement. I remember at one point I was working at Manly Swim Centre, which was outdoors, and for one winter helped work at The Forum, which was a horrible indoor pool in Collaroy and was later bulldozed for a set of apartments. The amount of chlorine in that pool was so bad that costumes faded quickly, swim caps disintegrated, and I remember that the hair that stuck out the bottom of my swim cap could be pulled straight from my head, without pain. The chlorine was so bad that it destroyed everything it touched! A new pair of swimming trunks would fade within one month.

At Manly there was one young girl, probably about 12 years-old, who had more energy than potentially even I had as a child. Now that's saying something. She may have even had as much energy as my now 9 year-old has (no, nobody has that much!). This young girl was hungry, passionate, and at 12, knew she wanted to be an Olympian. However I already knew this young girl because her Mum and my Aunt were best friends, and her older sister and my cousin were best friends (and they are still great friends to this day).

Elka Graham was her name. She was not the most talented of swimmers, but she had such a hunger and a dedication that I knew she was going to make it. Very few people can be that passionate and not make it, unless they simply lack the talent and need to change sports or activities. She went on to represent Australia and has now made a name for herself in TV and public speaking. I still feel proud to think I got to see a glimpse into how she made it to the top. And no, it wasn't my coaching that got her there, sadly. Okay, maybe just a little...

Even the talented can fail

On the opposite end of the spectrum was a young guy at The Forum. Let's call him James. When it comes to talent, this guy had it in spades. James was from a wealthy family, and it was very clear that everything was handed to him on a silver platter. His family ran a very successful business, he went to the top private school in the area, and it was apparent that he did not have to work for anything. He would do the bare minimum of training, yet still go to the State or National Titles and just blow the other swimmers out of the water. Not literally; he still actually had to get in the pool and swim against them…

I remember each morning he'd wander into training at 5am, along with the other swimmers and honestly, it would take twenty minutes to get him in the pool, and sometimes longer. He had zero interest in swimming. Even when he did get in, he would lazily swim up and down the pool, as if he was trying to infuriate me. I'd love to have told his mother this, but she was so snobbish that she wouldn't even talk to me, even though I was his swimming coach.

I remember having one conversation with him, saying, "James, you just have so much talent. You could make it all the way to the top, if you will just apply yourself at training." But my attempts to motivate him just went in one ear and out the other. I was never overly annoyed at him that he didn't take his swimming to the next level. It was just such a shame that he was so talented, yet it went to waste. As I write this I truly believe he could have been one of the greatest swimmers of all time. I'd been around enough talent by this time to understand just how good this kid was. He could have been in the league of Michael Phelps or Ian Thorpe, no doubt about it.

It was a great life lesson for me, again in observation. I learnt that it does not ultimately matter how much talent one has if they will not do the hard work. I saw many athletes who were not amazingly talented make it to the top because of their dedication, commitment and passion. I also learnt that when I would one day be a parent that if I had 'money', that I needed to watch the way my children were brought up. The aloofness of this mother left him thinking he was better than others and didn't have to work as hard as they do. This is fine while you're in the confines of the school world and Mum and Dad are bankrolling you, but it can set you up for a major fail in the real world when you're out there all alone, against people without privilege who have the hunger and determination to make something of their lives. Many of the ultra-successful have come from the 'wrong side of the tracks' because they're driven to make their life different.

I also learnt how I would never act if I was well off. No matter how much money I do or don't have, I will never treat another person as beneath me. If you're life is all about money then be careful. Proverbs 23:5 says:

"In the blink of an eye wealth disappears, for it will sprout wings and fly away like an eagle." NLT

In fact sometimes I feel my heart goes out more to people who are under-privileged and did not grow up with the opportunities or the training on life and money and business in their home. When I see someone pushing trolleys at the shopping centre, or doing other seemingly tedious jobs, I feel so proud for the fact that they are out there working hard, earning a living, as opposed to sitting back trying to work out how the government can support them via welfare.

To this day my wife and I walk that fine line with our children. We want them to grow up knowing who they are, but we also want to be sure that we give them that ability to fight a little for what they want. They are starting to understand what we do, and they see that Mum and Dad have a lot of responsibility. We talk about our success, how hard we work and how much we trust in God. A pastor friend of mine says to his kids, "Do your best, and God will do the rest." I have adopted it for our children, but also for ourselves. If we each get up each day and work hard, pray hard and give it our best shot, we can then hand our lives and dreams over to God, knowing that He can open doors, make connections and bring opportunities that are supernatural.

The point again is that, without passion, you're wasting your time. So if there is just one message that you can take out of this book, it is to **do what you are passionate about**. Don't do what others say you should; do the thing that brings you the most joy. By 'joy' I don't mean getting lost on the waves all day in surfing, or trying to do as little work as possible so you can travel the globe. I mean passion for your life calling; that one thing that keeps you up at night. The dream that if you could do anything, you would do this one thing.

You're only going to get one shot at life, so get dreaming – but most of all, get doing!

Tolerance consists of seeing certain things with your heart instead of your eyes.
ORLANDO A. BATTISTA

CHAPTER SEVEN

TIME TO GET SERIOUS

It was time to work on my next plan of attack, and so a trip to Europe helped me to re-focus. While I was away I used the brain space to think about my future. I knew it was going to be in business, but now to find out what area of business I should focus my energy on. Being overseas and seeing how big the world is helped open my young eyes to opportunity. I started to understand how the triathlon 'scene' worked, and as such I started to spot gaps in the multisport area. This was a growing market and one that I thought I could get a start in. I was also exceptionally passionate about it, as I thoroughly enjoyed everything about the health and fitness lifestyle. After a lifetime of living on the beach, I wanted to get away from the surfing world. It still involved the beach lifestyle, but in a whole new, disciplined way.

A friend who I competed in triathlons with and I approached a local surf club about staging a biathlon (a swim/run/swim event). Long story short, the surf club agreed, subject to them receiving a flat fee for staging the event, with us free to keep any profits over and above this. We used their insurance, their venue and their lifesavers for water safety, but the event was ours. It was a massive success, and I still recall counting up the cash and working out the profit that Sunday afternoon. And it was impressive. But more than that, it was invigorating. Seeing hundreds of people on the beach that morning, with the buzz of the commentator, the water safety crew, the spectators and so on was exciting – and slightly terrifying.

The adrenalin rush of event management is huge, but more than that, there is a whole lot of business that needs to go on behind the scenes to make the event happen. There were sponsorship proposals to write and present, council to meet with, surf club meetings to get the event over the line, entry forms to design and distribute, and so on. And it was pre the days where council costs and legislation, as well as insurance costs, had not yet ballooned. Now, the sun has set a little on that business; the ship has sailed and it is a very difficult business jut based on the red tape around the running of events.

There is of course, still money to be made, but it is a very mature market, and as the big media companies are seeing their revenue decline and are thus moving into the event world, it is getting ultra-competitive. But these were the early days where councils were happy to have events in their area and events were fairly easy to get approval on. In this age of litigation, it is now a risk-laden business.

This is where I finally realized that I was meant to be a businessman. Sitting at a desk with a phone and computer: this was not work, this was more fun than anything I had ever done before. The idea of going to university or further study was shelved. I just knew I had it in me to make it in business.

My friend who was involved with the biathlon only did the one-off event with me before moving back into his main job as a builder. He was about 12 years older and had a successful building business with his Dad, so I decided to set up my own business. I went on to run a range of events, including a half marathon, a triathlon and duathlon (run/bike/run for the winter months) series, plus a few different fun runs. It was a profitable little business and enjoyable for a time, but it was not the end game. I learned a lot running events, but it's also highly stressful and highly vulnerable. It could be as little as bad weather and an event's entries could drop by a half. The work was all weekend and the events weren't evenly spaced out, so managing the irregular cash flow was a whole new challenge for me.

Summer is a profitable season for an events business, but with a much leaner winter schedule, you had to be very careful you didn't spend all your money in the good months, with nothing to tie you over for the bad. For a young guy who had little responsibility, that was fine, but by now, I was a man of the world. I was a mortgage holder. I had a commitment to pay the bank back each and every month, so I had to be careful that the businesses I was in now had consistent cash flow throughout the year. Ahh, the overwhelming responsibilities of a 21 year-old…

Humphreys
Events were fun, but advertising was expensive and publishing was still the area that I wanted to pursue. Publishing was the business that could keep me awake at night, dreaming about the

future. And hey, this was pre-Internet days. If you owned the presses, you controlled the news. As a publisher, the advertisers beat a path to your door because if they wanted to get to that particular market, you as the publisher had the eyeballs of those people. You were very influential, so if you're a triathlon organizer and you want to promote your summer series to triathletes, then you simply had to advertise in the triathlon magazines. This is the same across any industry that needs exposure. Therefore, publishers were very powerful, and many were very rich.

During this time one of my fascinations was going down to Humphreys Newsagency in Manly Beach, Sydney. Humphreys was the largest newsstand in the southern hemisphere and there was literally not a magazine printed in English that they didn't stock. I could stand in Humphreys for hours at a time – and I mean hours – dreaming of the magazines that I could own. And as Huphreys was smack in the middle of Manly Corso, one of the busiest tourist beaches in all of Sydney, I was not offending the store owners by not buying anything. The store was always packed, to the point where Humphreys had security staff to watch that the product was not being stolen by all of the tourists. These were the days when Rupert Murdoch and Kerry Packer ruled the world. Who wouldn't want to be in media?

The dream was too big... for now
So I set off with my plan to make it happen, but I was in for a surprise... I came up with an idea for a running magazine. I spotted a nice gap in the market and knew there were enough apparel and footwear companies, not to mention nutritional suppliers and event organizers, to sell the advertising to cover

the cost of printing. Where should I start? Producing the actual magazine would not be an issue – pardon the pun. If you can run triathlons and the like, with hundreds of people needing to be registered, roads to be closed and for the race to be successful for that many competitors, then producing a magazine would be much simpler in comparison. Plus it was 9am to 5pm; no crazy hours and weekend work, but rather office hours, leaving the weekends and evenings free for leisure. What's not to like?

The first step was selecting the specifications on my magazine and from there I contacted the printers, requesting quotes. This was getting exciting. I was starting to think of the cover designs, the editorial and the marketing. I'd already worked a plan where all the back issues (the unsold copies of each issue) would be distributed through all the different fun runs and triathlons across the country. The competitors would get a free magazine, the event organizers would be providing their customers, many who pay good money to enter an event, with something for nothing, and advertisers would benefit from having their brand exposed to the athletes all over the country.

Unfortunately my dream would need to wait a while longer before coming to pass. Again, showing how long ago this was, the first print quote arrived in the mail (yes, the snail mail). The price per issue came in at – wait for it... $33,000. My excitement quickly evaporated as I looked at these numbers. Sadly quotes two and three were not much better and as I rechecked the figures, I realized that magazine publishing, while still being my desire, may be a few years off yet. I just didn't have the business skills to be responsible for that sort of money. Every month. No wonder the publishers were the really rich guys: they were the only ones who had the money to play at that level, and across multiple titles as well.

Owning the presses

From there my dream was to own print presses. I figured that if I owned the presses, then I would be free to print what I wanted, as my clients would be paying for the running of them. I once again set about doing a lot of due diligence on trying to make this happen, including meetings with companies that sell printing presses. Magazines, being full colour, are printed on very expensive presses, and as such it was going to cost hundreds of thousands of dollars to set up a printing factory, with all the machinery necessary to print at that high level.

This was much more than just a pipedream though. In my mind I had it set that I was going to be the next Rupert Murdoch or Kerry Packer. In reality it was a ridiculous dream. These guys ran public companies; massive operations with hundreds of millions (in Rupert's case, it ran into the billions) in bank funding. They were at a level that few others were at.

But I have never let small details like that stop me. I have always dreamt big and stepped out in faith. If I have known God was with me, and that it was a 'God idea', as opposed to a good idea, then I dream big, get working on my plan, and let God help fill in the gaps along the way. Living a life of faith can be frightening at times, and while it is not for the faint-hearted, it really is an exhilarating life.

In fact this might sound random, but one of my favorite little books for my kids is the Dr Seuss book *Oh The Places You'll Go*. Here is just a quick snippet:

"You're off to Great Places!
Today is your day!
Your mountain is waiting,
So... get on your way!"

"So be sure when you step, Step with care and great tact. And remember that life's A Great Balancing Act. And will you succeed? Yes! You will, indeed! (98 and ¾ percent guaranteed) Kid, you'll move mountains."

"You'll get mixed up, of course, as you already know. You'll get mixed up with many strange birds as you go. So be sure when you step. Step with care and great tact and remember that Life's a Great Balancing Act. Just never forget to be dexterous and deft. And never mix up your right foot with your left."

"Oh the places you'll go! There is fun to be done! There are points to be scored. There are games to be won. And the magical things you can do with that ball will make you the winning-est winner of all."

A brilliant book. If you don't buy it for your children, buy it for yourself. Plus you'll be happy to know this book was published by Rupert Murdoch's company, Harper Collins.

Back to the presses. Again, without going into too much detail, this was simply not going to happen. Being a printer was probably harder than being a publisher. Equipment was expensive, you needed a whopping factory, vey experienced staff to operate the presses, and so this was not an option. But I was proud of myself that I was once again thinking outside the square. I wasn't just taking no for an answer; I was looking for ways to circumnavigate what in the natural seemed impossible. I've always believed that we need to think outside the square, to find another way. There is always another way, and it's your job to dig and find it.

Too many people just accept the status quo. They run with the crowd, they swim with the tide, but I believe it is our job to swim upstream; to not listen and believe everything we are told. To dream a big dream, an impossible dream, and then you work with God on how the two of you are going to bring it to pass.

> You can't see an awful lot
> by looking in a rear-view mirror.
> ROBERT SKELTON

CHAPTER EIGHT

THE CHICKEN ROLL TRANSFORMATION

As a young man, like most in business, I was struggling with cash flow between growing tired of my events business, while working on my next project. With a mortgage to pay, I wanted a little extra each week so I could keep the profits in the business, but at the same time still be able to enjoy life. I wanted work though that would not interrupt my day, so I found a job where I could start at 5am and be finished by 8.30am, giving me a full day to work. The job was delivering pre-made sandwiches and chicken rolls, wrapped in plastic, to service/gas stations across the city. It was four mornings per week.

This is also where I also developed my love of coffee. Because this was a regular delivery run, I got to know most of the customers quite well. Calling on them a few mornings a week at an hour when they were quiet meant I got to have a quick chat before they got busy for the day. At one of the car washes on the south side of Sydney, near the airport, I met a nice guy and it wasn't long before he began to ask me if I'd like a cup of coffee. At first I said yes, just to be polite, but as time went on, that morning coffee really got me out of bed. Prior to this a strawberry milkshake was my go-to drink if I was out at a café, but once I got that taste for coffee, I never looked back.

I also looked a bit more sophisticated going to meetings drinking coffee, as opposed to strawberry milkshakes. I guess in business perception is everything... But where this really transformed my life was the prayer time that I got. Listening to music or talkback radio for 3-4 hours drove me slightly insane, so I used the time to pray. I found myself driving around the streets of Sydney in the dark speaking the Word of God over my life. As I did I could feel my spirit growing. Each morning I would start my day literally making up a hit-list of scriptures that would build my faith. I was attending a local church called C3 Oxford Falls – or at the time known as Christian City Church Oxford Falls – and the pastor, Phil Pringle, was an absolute man of faith.

He was a visionary and what he said, he did. He developed a lot of respect from his church members because not only did he talk big, but he backed it up by following through on what he said he would do. Years later, if there is one thing that I admire about Ps Phil, is the fact that he pushed people to dream big, all the while biting off a very big vision himself, and then having to achieve this in the public domain. Accordingly there were a lot of business people in the church; lots of big-thinkers who would not normally attend church, but who could see that the man on the stage had at least the same drive – and most likely higher levels of faith – as they did.

Ps Phil had personally built his faith through the Word of

God, and the very scriptures that he used in his own life were the same that he would quote to the congregation. Some of those included:
- *"Fear not for I am with you says the Lord."* Isaiah 41:10
- *"Enlarge the place of your tent, stretch your tent curtains wide, do not hold back; lengthen your cords, strengthen your stakes."* Isaiah 54:2
- *"I can do all things through Christ who strengthens me."* Philippians 4:13
- *"Now to Him who is able to do exceedingly abundantly above all that we ask or think, according to the power that works in us..."* Ephesians 3:20

He was up at 5.30am every morning, walking the beach and ensuring he got his time with God. I got to know these same scriptures well and they became the backbone to my Christian living. They say that the word a preacher preaches is as much for him as for his congregation, so with the level of faith Ps Phil needed to keep his organization running smoothly financially, let alone emotionally and spiritually, he would quote positive scripture after scripture, Sunday after Sunday. This just became an amazing way of life for me.

To this day, I feel exceptionally grateful that I was able to grow up in such an atmosphere of faith. I was not just in church, but rather part of a faith-filled environment where it was normal to expect that with God, literally anything was possible. So on this morning sandwich run, I really took my faith to a new level. At a time when most people would still be in bed – I definitely would have been – I was instead driving around Sydney in that van, quoting scripture after scripture, building inside me the faith that I would need to do God's work.

Dreaming wide awake

I had always prayed that God would have my life; that it was His to do as He wanted with it, and I was never worried to offer it up to Him. By this time, I had found that God spoke to me through dreams and visions. Not the dreams while I was asleep, but in visions and dreams when I was awake. I could see my life planned out, and the more time I spent with Him, the more I knew where I was going, and felt an excitement in the direction He was leading me.

Many people are nervous about giving their lives to God, worried that He will make them do the exact opposite of what they want to. For example, if your dream was to be an artist, he would take that from you and was certain to make you miserable on the mission field. If your dream was to be a missionary, then you'd find yourself instead working in retail. If you dreamt of being a businessman, then God would instead make you a preacher. If the dream was a preacher, surely he'd put you in cold-call sales. You get the picture. I know this is how many people in the church feel. They are too scared to give God their whole life for fear that He'll suck the dream out of them. It is devastating because we have churches full of bored Christians; people just living week to week, without seeing anything amazing happening in their world because they are too afraid to give their dreams over to God. As a Christian, that is no way to live.

Even now I don't know or understand where this mindset comes from, (actually, I do have a clue…) but in my mind it is totally a false doctrine. The Bible clearly says in Psalm 37:4:

"Delight yourself in the Lord and He will give you the desires of your heart."

So that scripture alone totally cancels out the fact that God is the ultimate kill-joy, just waiting to suck the vision, passion and excitement for life out of His people. The other point I should clarify here is that often we have a dream and a vision, and while it excites us, it is not ultimately what we are called to do. So if you do give your life over to Him in full and He in fact has something else for you to do, don't fear. God will put a new desire in your heart, one that will cancel out the one you had.

Many times I have seen this in my own life. I have been excited by something, only to realize it is not ultimately what God is wanting. But every time he replaces it with something better. So I can now trust Him that if He closes a door in one area, it is because he is going to open an even better one elsewhere. But it is developing that maturity in God where He has your whole life. And that's why only a small percentage of Christians end up living in that place of really seeing amazing things happen, as ultimately there is only a small percentage who are confident enough to really give God their entire lives.

Developing my prayer life

That platform for prayer has been with me ever since. I didn't have that sandwich job for long. About six months, I think, but it was transformational in both my prayer and faith life. The platform of prayer and faith had been firmly set. I got very busy in my next business, direct marketing, and no longer needed that additional income, but I found my prayer life really continued on and it was walking that cemented my ability to hear God's voice clearly. This represented a major change in my life, as prior to this point, I had not been able to walk anywhere. I couldn't even walk down the street; I would have to jog as I just didn't have the patience to walk.

I walked those streets slowly talking to God – and Hearing His voice. It felt like the longer I walked, the more I could connect with God and distinctly hear what I felt He was trying to tell me. God is always wanting to talk to us, but if we cannot find the time to listen to Him, then many of the amazing things He wants to tell you will not be revealed. It's a still small voice, not an over-powering one, and so if the TV is on, you're on social media, or doing anything where you cannot sit or think quietly, chances are you will miss hearing His voice.

For those who don't want to go to new levels in both God and life, this may not be so important, but for those with the desire to really see something amazing happen, it is a pre-requisite. However, it is getting harder to do. Back when I built that discipline of a prayer life, there was no email on my phone to distract me. There was no Facebook or social media, and no constant digital entertainment to keep stealing my attention. Even now I have to be really disciplined to walk and not check emails. They are coming in all the time, and so many of them for work seem to demand our constant, immediate attention. It is hard; we all have that slight – or major – social media addiction, and this can seriously affect us in just turning everything off and spending quality time with God.

You know, from all those years of spending time driving/walking and praying with God, you would think that by now the base had been laid and that I could pull back in prayer. In most things in life, once you've truly done the 'hard yards', you can ease off the accelerator a little and build some lifestyle in to what you do, as the hard work in the previous years now drives the momentum for you. But not so with prayer.

The Bible says in 1Peter 5:8 that the devil is like a roaring lion, constantly trying to devour. This is a daily fight – and I mean daily. I have put him in his place daily over the years, using the Word of God to fight the devil's lies for my life, my family and my business that you'd think by now he'd be in his place and would go and find someone else to hassle. But that's not the way it works. He pushes the same lies at me, day after day, doing his best to break me.

The daily battle

While I totally have him in place in my life – that is, he clearly knows that he is a defeated foe; that greater is He in me than he in the world; that I simply resist the devil and he will flee from me; that no weapon formed against me shall prosper – it does not mean that daily he does not try and bring the same lies and insults to my door. Each morning I wake up and in prayer put him in his place. How do I do that? By counteracting his lies with the Word of God: *"My God shall supply all my needs"* (Philippians 4:19); *"I am blessed coming in and blessed going out"* (Deuteronomy 28:6); *"I am the head and not the tail, above and not beneath"* (Deuteronomy 28:13); *"Delight yourself in the Lord and He will give you the desires of your heart"* (Psalm 37:4); *"I will bless those who bless you, and curse those who curse you"* (Genesis 12:3).

I have to fight daily to retain that position. Fighting with the

Word of God is how you do it. It distinguishes his strategy, as the Word of God is sharper than a two-edged sword.

I fear sometimes that some Christians are scared of the devil. The messages of how he comes to "kill, steal and destroy"; how he "walks around like a roaring lion" can seem terrifying if they are not put into context as to the power we have over the enemy. I learnt a very important lesson about the devil when I was about 18 years of age. I was at a house church that was coincidentally run by my brother-in-law when he explained the way the devil plied his trade.

"The devil is like a toothless lion," he explained. "All he has is a loud roar. But to we who are saved and come under the name of Jesus Christ, he cannot get near us." I am not sure if those words changed the lives of the others in that room that night, but they certainly did so for me. All the devil has is that roar, and to those who don't understand the power they have over the devil, it could be frightening. It's a loud roar, nonetheless. Intimidation is one of his keys. If he can leave you frightened to move forward in your life into the things that God is calling you into, then he has done his job.

He is not just intimidating you on your big dreams. It could be freaking a young guy out about getting married, and the responsibilities he will need to take on. From the smallest things, right through to your big dreams, if he can leave you in fear and worry about the future, then you'll be safer if you do nothing. When we have a church world doing nothing, then we are an impotent body. I have always marveled how so many in business can have the faith to step out into the deep unknown when they don't have God beside them. Many launch out seriously deep, too, so if they can do it with no safety net of a loving father to guide them, surely we who have the King of Kings as the Lord of our lives should be stepping into greater levels.

Only a couple of years ago I was talking to a pastor friend who was telling me how so many Christians end up living impotent lives because of this. They want to move forward and dream big dreams, but then feel that that would be wrong (the devil's input here). They want to build an investment portfolio that would see them in a good financial position and would set up future generations, but then hear the stories that the love of money is the root of all evil, and so they don't proceed. They have dreams and visions, those things that keep them up late at night, but surely it is their job on earth to 'pick up their Cross' for God and get their treasure in heaven, not earth, and so we see a church that is totally confused; worried to step out in to greater things because of worry that they are not living the life God wants them to. But then we wonder why the church is in decline, why Christians seem so 'vanilla' in their lives. Seriously, would you want to join? As I mentioned earlier, we need to be front and centre in the marketplace.

I am not just referring to business here. In our church, there is a wonderful family, (actually there are many wonderful families and individuals). The husband is a chef in one of the better restaurants in Noosa and his wife, who has always had a dream of being a doctor, finally in her forties decided to pursue her dream. That meant this family would go from two incomes to one, but it was a price they were prepared to pay for her to fulfil her dream.

How inspiring that these guys were putting what they heard

in church each week into practice in their lives. What a rich life that makes for when you step out and follow your dreams.

These guys counted the cost; they did their homework to ensure their family could survive financially during this long course of study. Would it be safer to stay where they were? You bet. But they decided to put legs on their faith and put it to work. Soon after they stepped out, the husband was made redundant. Now their faith was really on the line. However, God stepped in and provided him with an even better job. They just stood on the Word of God and trusted, and God came through, as He always does.

Because I went to such a faith-filled church, I just thought that that was the way all churches were. I was young, filled with faith, and the attendees of the church were encouraged to get out there and live their best life. I thought that that was how Christianity worked; I thought that was how most churches were. So as you read this, I urge you to take a totally different look at God. He put you on this earth for a unique purpose, and not to be a vanilla follower of His. He even gave us the parable of the talents (Matthew 25:14-30) to back up what I am saying.

If I am wrong in my theology here, then why was the one who buried his talent the one that was chastised? He should have been the one that was praised. Those that put their hand to the plough and produced a return should have been scorned for being too worldly, or commercially-minded. Thank you, Ps Phil Pringle, that you saved me a life of misery by not setting me up with the beliefs that Christians should live mediocre lives. You have forever changed my life, my wife and children's lives and I pray many others outside of your church as I take this message

THE CHICKEN ROLL TRANSFORMATION

out into the marketplace.

Our church leaders also need to take a look at their beliefs surrounding God, money, His call on peoples' lives and so on, as it is the pastors that have the ears of their parishoners every week that have the ability to speak life into these people. If you're a small-thinking pastor, then it's hard to create world-changers within your church. So we need pastors who get it. And I know what you're thinking: this opens the door for our churches to be all about money, success and earthly possessions. And you are right. If this area is not handled with the greatest balance and wisdom, then it does not take a lot for it to tip to the other end of the scale and then the church just blends into the world. It's a very fine line and I am thankful it is not an issue I have to confront in not being a pastor. But still, it's 2018, and the church cannot operate like it's 1984 and get away with it. We need pastors, missionaries and evangelists, but that is for three percent of the Christian population. The other 97% can be world changers in their industries, influencing the marketplace on a daily basis for Christ. Remember, you only get one shot in this life, so why not make it a good one?

So on with the story…

If you are pleased at finding faults,
you are displeased at finding perfections.
JOHANN LAVATER

CHAPTER NINE

HITTING THE WALL

I cannot be sure how I fell into it, but direct marketing became a major business for me. If there were two industries that I really enjoyed, it was direct marketing and media. Media was some way off, as mentioned, and so direct marketing was a business that I was really interested in. Part of the interest was for the cash flow it created. If you bring a great product into to market and then proceed down the path of wholesale, then the drain on your cash flow is phenomenal. But if you were able to sell direct to the consumer, where they pay you in advance, then there is the ability to run a cash flow positive operation.

Finding the right products was always the challenge and then trying to find suppliers who already had the stock so that I could purchase from them as I needed it was the next stumbling block. But as I dug I found such suppliers and consequently I didn't need to buy all our stock from offshore. Mind you, many product lines still had to be imported. Some key suppliers were local, leaving me free to concentrate on the marketing, not having to carry the high cost of the stock as well.

I took to this business pretty easily and it was successful quickly. My biggest challenge was the cost of advertising. Full page ads in the major TV guides inserted inside the Sunday newspapers, or ads in magazines like *New Idea* and *Woman's Day* could be up to $12,000 for a full page ad for just one week's exposure. So for a young guy in his mid-twenties to be running these was a pretty big deal. But run them I did, and successful I was. It got to the point where I ended up setting up a warehouse with a guy I had gone to school with. He and his girlfriend moved out to Sydney's far western suburbs – that's right, they were now ultra-westies – and through the business they were running had a warehouse.

They were struggling to get their product into the market, so Ken agreed to be our fulfillment centre and as the orders were processed at my end, we could courier all of the invoices out to Windsor daily. The stock was all ordered and sent to Windsor, Ken and his girlfriend did all the pick and pack, the orders all shipped on our shipping account with the courier companies, and we were a well-oiled machine. We also hired a software engineer to build a mail order system specifically tailored to what we were doing. Every single ad, whether in print or TV, had a special code, so as our orders were keyed in at data entry, we not only saw the sales, but we could add in the cost of the ad. We had a quick profit and loss on every ad spend, meaning we could accurately work out the sales from every ad right down to the last dollar, and we thus knew whether to repeat the ad or not.

It was a highly stressful business, as I was spending a fortune weekly on advertising. The thing that made the business work for us was that the customers paid in advance. Their cash payments meant we always had the capital to buy the stock and pay for the advertising. We used TV and magazines as our two main channels, but I found that magazine advertising worked best for us. As most people paid by check (cheque) in the mail, we did not need lots of phone staff to handle the rush of calls that you need if you're in the TV market. Some days so many orders came through the mail that we could not even get them all entered into the software. It was incredible.

I remember taking a call from my ad rep at one of the big publishing houses. There were two major magazine publishers in Australia: one owned by Kerry Packer, the other, Pacific Magazines, by the largest printing company in Australia. And it was the latter that we did the majority of our business with. They just had the magazines, *New Idea* being one of them, that seemed to fit for us. Incidentally Pacific Magazines is now owned by Kerry Stokes, one of Australia's richest men.

I called our ad rep saying that the most I would pay for a page was $7000; to not call me unless he had a deal. Amazingly (sarcasm used here) every week he had a special $7,000 deal, just for me... Given a full page was $12,000, we were getting a pretty steep discount. These were heady days for a young man.

For the first time in my life I was really learning to manage some big dollars. What this business venture did for me was show me that I really had a knack for business. When you are young, (and back then business was an older man's domain) you had to have deep pockets to be in business. Otherwise people tended to walk all over you. It was has hard to be taken seriously. It was difficult to get respect from the big players. There was no digital business; he (or she) with the deepest pockets would win and I was competing against major direct marketing companies, most of them US owned. Somehow I managed to carve out a major niche. I was dealing with the big players of the publishing game and proving I had what it takes. I was developing an inner confidence in me that whatever I put my hands to, I could achieve.

I recall taking a girl from church on a date one evening. I picked her up and as we were driving to dinner that Friday evening I remember thinking to myself, "How many other 25 year-olds have a business that just recorded $38,000 in sales that week?" Not many I suspect, and with no debt and only minimal capital ever invested into the business, this was not too bad an effort. Around this time I also really started to get excited by publishing again. If only I owned the magazines my ads were in, then I wouldn't just be making the publisher rich. I was beginning to get excited about creating a plan for getting into media. And now I felt I had the confidence in dealing with larger sums of money to be able to make it happen.

Franklin Mint, the massive American mail order company of the day, were the category-killers of mail order. You could barely open a magazine anywhere without seeing one of their full page ads. They had the back page of most of the major weekly women's magazines, like *New Idea*, *Woman's Day*, *Take 5* and *That's Life*. They also used to have multiple ads in the TV magazines that were inserted inside the Sunday newspapers, and because this was just pre-Internet days, everyone bought the Sunday paper so they knew what was on the TV for the week.

In Sydney alone, the two Sunday newspapers would have been selling 1.5 million Sunday editions. *Woman's Day* was selling around 750,000 copies weekly, *New Idea* around 495,000 weekly, and so these were big magazines with massive reach. This was pretty serious business for a young man. But it also makes you soon realize why Rupert Murdoch and Kerry Packer were so rich.

This was no business for a young man in his early to mid-twenties, but I just went for it – and it worked. Filming commercials, designing print ads and seeing a bag full of mail coming in to the post office each day was pretty exciting stuff. I was not married, did not have a girlfriend at the time, and so I could devote my life to business. The post office advised that we had to change our mailing address from a post office box to a locked bag, as the volume of mail we received had to be placed in a hessian sack each day.

I remember the day I felt like I had made it. A customer had accidentally sent a check to Franklin Mint instead of my company for one of our products. They had not included our address, or coupon, as it was known, but Franklin Mint had known the address details of our company to forward it on to us. I was shocked. A massive American competitor knew who we were and how to get our mail to us. For a young man, this was a big deal. Franklin Mint was owned by Time Warner, so they had slightly deeper pockets than me...

Pride comes before the fall

Direct marketing is fickle and as such I ended up with some products that were not selling. As mentioned, advertising in direct marketing is probably your highest cost, on par with the cost of stock, and unfortunately I got caught out. I started to see some of our most popular products slowing and so I was frantically trying to launch new products to find the next big seller. However, I couldn't find one, and when you're burning $7,000 per ad, it can be an expensive way of testing the market.

The ad bills kept coming in, but the sales didn't follow suit. When I finally lifted my head and realized I needed to do something about this, I had run up a sizeable, six-figure debt. Maybe I wasn't quite as good as I thought I was. This was the age that I really grew up. I was determined that I was not going to go under though. I made contact with the publishers, TV stations and suppliers that I owed money to and worked out a payment plan with each of them.

The stress was unbearable, as at the time I had no way of paying them back. Thankfully, for all of the time I had spent praying, I knew that somehow, some way, God would help me through. There were no banks involved and so my creditors accepted my terms. That was a relief, but now to find how to pay back what I owed. I might also add that my 'terms' were not in reducing the amount owed to each creditor, but just extending the period in which each would be paid.

One of the reasons I felt the door close on this business is that it is an industry that really trades on – in my opinion – deceit. Really, the products are over-sold, or exceptionally exaggerated, and I often felt uncomfortable selling some of the products we did. I knew that this was not what God had for me long-term, but again, I learnt so much more about business, as well as the power of advertising and marketing. Even to this day I'll watch infomercials on TV, or see print ads, and I clearly know all of the direct marketing tricks that make a very average product a must-have. Add to this an easy payment plan, the-first-37-callers-receive-a-free-additional-product, or 'call in the next 20 minutes

(20 minutes from when) to receive a special [insert here] gift' and you can see how easy it is to create demand and hype for something pretty average. But it's a formula that works, and the big direct marketing companies can ship container loads of very ordinary products every week.

Many businesses see advertising and marketing as an expense; a waste of valuable income that is then washed away, but then they wonder why there is low demand for their product or service. I saw first hand how powerful advertising is. Our phones and mail literally ceased when we stopped advertising.

> **Blessed are the young,
> for they shall inherit the national debt.**
> HERBERT HOOVER

CHAPTER TEN

TIME TO CLEAR MY DEBTS

I sought God for six weeks straight on what I should do. This next venture was crucial. It simply had to work, as there was so much money to pay back. This was night and day stuff, under massive pressure, waiting on the Lord for my next steps. It was also winter, so the weather was cold and miserable, making me feel even more depressed about my situation. I remember going to church, barbeques, parties and so on and mixing with other guys my age thinking, "You have no idea the pressures I am facing." Generally speaking, men of 25 to 26 years of age were not operating businesses the size that I was running, and while I also learnt business skills that they hadn't, I lost a valuable time of my life, given the pressure I was under. This was a stage of life where I should have been having a ton of fun, but instead I was carrying responsibilities well beyond my age.

Lord, give me a sign

I knew absolutely nothing about the Internet, except for the fact that it was the future – and it was where I needed to be, but I had to move fast, as I was getting semi-daily calls from creditors waiting on their next installment. So while I was under the pump, I also had to wait for God's clear guidance. As I walked the streets and beach for hours on end in waiting to hear from Him I clearly remember Him showing me that this was the next step. When I got the idea, I knew it was from God. I just had that inner peace that I had an answer. However, I still put it to God to test that this was definitely from Him.

A guy from church, Peter Kelaher, had become a good friend of mine. He was going to be the perfect gauge as to whether this was a good idea or not. He was about six years older, but was a great salesman and started a successful business as a real estate buyer. He was first to market in Sydney, buying property on behalf of time-poor, wealthy business executives. He was also pretty strong-willed and opinionated, never afraid to tell me – or anyone else – what he really thought. But it was done in love, not aggression, and so I really did value his honest, forthright opinions. He had an amazing heart for people and was a fantastic evangelist.

We were due to catch up for a surf and coffee one Saturday afternoon, and so I went to the Lord and said, "God, if this idea is truly from you, then I am going to share it with Pete, and in detail, so he can pick it apart. If he thinks it is a good idea and worth pursuing, then it's all systems go. However if he rejects it, then that will be a sign that this is not from you."

This was a pretty crazy prayer for me, really putting God on

TIME TO CLEAR MY DEBTS

the spot. I met with Pete and he thought it was a great idea. I had the answer from God that I had sought.

A week or two earlier, our church had a conference and one of the big-name American speakers brought with him a very successful guy in his church. Our church organized a special breakout session for business people, where this guy was the main speaker. As he was talking he recounted the story of not knowing whether he was meant to stay in this business, or instead move across to ministry. He felt that tug in his heart between the two, so he took it to God and said, "God, I don't know which way to go and I need you to help me. Over the next 4 weeks, if my turnover falls under $2 million in any of those weeks (yes, he ran a major computer supply business), then this will be a sign that you're moving me into ministry. If it stays above that, then I'll know that is a sign that my calling really is in business, and thus I'll stay where I am."

He went on to tell the audience that in those four weeks he had record weeks of sales. Now I clearly understand how at this point, there will be some readers who don't agree with his methodology, and that's okay. However, I personally believe we serve a God who wants the best for our lives, who wants us positioned as to where we will best flourish and so is happy to answer His children's prayers. I don't believe He wants His children roaming around the earth in a perennial state of confusion. The Bible even says that a double-minded man is unstable in all his ways. (James 1:8) Plus, in my case, desperate times sought desperate measures!

Becoming an expert

So, back to the Internet. What do you do when you want to move into a brand new industry, but you know nothing about it? Simple: you write a book about it. That's what you do, right? Well, that's what I did. I didn't write it to get it published, though. Writers are experts on a subject, so I researched the Internet so thoroughly that I ended up having enough knowledge that I could start a fully-fledged web development company. As I was busy during the day getting the business ready, I was writing between 5am and 8am every morning. I remember it was winter, and so setting my alarm for 4.50am was exceptionally difficult to do. But I just knew that this is what I had to do to make this work. I had to learn the business, so I taught myself each aspect of the business by writing a book as though I was the authority on it.

I knew I'd be sitting in meetings with some very smart people. These same people would be seeing me as the net expert, and so there would be nowhere to hide. If I was going to win their business, I just had to know what I was talking about. I spent about 12 weeks writing this book. It was on everything from designing a website, to metatags, to search engine optimization, and more. I broke the book up into the chapters that I saw this new business operating in, and that way, whenever I'd be quizzed from a potential client, I would have on tap, access to information that would just roll off my tongue.

It worked. With my flair for marketing, I produced brochures that were professional and compelling, showing companies that the Internet was the future, and *we* knew the way there. This was around the turn of the century and every business owner knew

TIME TO CLEAR MY DEBTS

they needed to be on the net, even though most didn't really know why. Even I had no idea at the time just how much the net was going to transform our lives.

Did the book get published? Well, let me tell you, it went very close. I submitted it to a company called McGraw-Hill, a major business publisher, just to see how I'd go. I figured that if I went to the trouble of writing it, then it was certainly worth submitting it to see what they thought of it. In the end they wanted to publish a few chapters of it as part of a compilation. There were a few 'experts' in various elements of the web, so they wanted a 'best of the best' style of book for the market. I ended up saying I wasn't interested, which at the time, I wasn't. The aim was to write it to learn the industry, not get published. Had they accepted the full manuscript I would have gone for it. Looking back I was crazy not to have accepted. I would have been a published author 17 years earlier with more than just a business card to show potential clients!

God's connections, though, are amazing. One night I ended up at the house of a guy in my church. He was taking on a new product, wanted to set up a sales team, and had three of us that he wanted to join him as directors in his new company. Whilst I did not go on to take up his offer, one of the other guys was a Chinese-Australian man who had started a web development firm. I got his card, arranged to meet him for a coffee, and it was agreed that his firm would do all of the work that my firm brought in. It proved very successful. He and his team were more on the technical end than the sales end, whereas I was always very comfortable meeting, talking and selling to people.

So while we were winning the work, Ernie's company was

doing the work, and we were both prospering. This brought me into some pretty powerful boardrooms, and I remember winning the job to re-develop the website for NTT Docomo, Japan's biggest telecommunications company. I also started writing for the B2B advertising magazine *B&T Weekly*, the prestigious advertising trade magazine of the day, which made me a sort-of expert. I'd always bring a couple of copies to key meetings to show the potential client I wrote for a powerful magazine. But it was back to basic supply and demand. There was huge demand, and we were there ready to supply.

Within one year all debts were paid and we had a great clientele. It was a frustrating period though as I was working tirelessly, but didn't make a cent, as all money went to my creditors. What's that Bible scripture about the borrower being slave to the lender?

I must tell you a funny story though. This was the first time in my life that I was going into boardrooms of major companies in the central business district and it was a little surreal. With one of my sales guys, we had a meeting with a major publishing company who were pitching their web work. It was a very cordial meeting and their marketing manager and the other few people that attended the meeting escorted us out and into the foyer on the entrance level of the building. It was a beautiful, big foyer with massive glass panels. As we said our goodbyes and shook hands, my sales guy somehow thought there wasn't a door and walked straight into the glass at pace, before falling backwards onto the ground.

Everyone in the foyer, including those from the meeting, watched on, feeling ever so embarrassed for him. That was the end of the meeting and sadly we never did hear from them again. We must have made a lasting impression… As we walked out the door I knew that was one client we were not going to land.

All the while though, in the back of my mind, was the fact that I was just a surfer from the Northern Beaches of Sydney. What was I doing trying to mix with the business elite? This was something that I had to really work hard to overcome in business: to know that I was at the same level of these corporate guys was hard for me to get my head around. I was a young guy mixing with the top end of town. I was also wearing a suit, something foreign to me, but from a standing start, I was in the boardrooms of some very powerful people, helping them work out their web strategies.

This not only gave me the confidence to play at a high level, but it also showed me how normal the people in these positions were. At every level of business, people are trying to figure out what is next. I was as smart as them. I was probably a lot more experienced in actually being a business owner and not being employed by a corporation, with the financial safety net that brings, and so I became a lot less intimidated.

This reminds me of a documentary I watched on Rupert Murdoch. Based in Britain early on in his career and copping it from all sides for being in their country and taking over their newspapers, he earned the nickname the 'Dirty Digger'. He said to his wife, "I don't like the 'Establishment.'"

She replied to him, "Rupert, you are the Establishment."

We need to know our place in God: that we are the head and not the tail, and to not be intimidated by the so-called experts. It was God showing me that He will open the doors, that He will make the connections. That I *do* in fact have what it takes.

Publishing remained the end game for me. As a really interesting side note though, as I have previously mentioned I used to have a dream of owning my own presses so that I could print my own magazines and while that dream 'failed' to eventuate, it's interesting to see how God works. Because of the web experience we had gained in running our own web business, this put us in the perfect position to in fact own our own 'digital presses'. With the Internet skill set that now exists within the walls of Initiate Media, there is really no project that we cannot undertake. And God has the best way. Rather than the risk and cost of running physical presses, the Internet gives us the ability to spread the Word of God around the world. Literally. So when you get these crazy God ideas, sometimes they might not be quite as crazy as you might think. They might pan out differently to what you are expecting, but just go with it.

> The cynic never grows up,
> but commits intellectual suicide.
> CHARLES R BROWN

CHAPTER ELEVEN

THE WORLD OF PUBLISHING

Finally, I had the money behind me to give publishing a go. I could test the market and make some mistakes, as I had the money from the web business to pay the bills. So off we went. We got started with a triathlon magazine, followed by running and ultimately followed by business. We had three magazines in our stable by the time I was 29. Life was pretty good, if not easy. I was learning the challenging ropes of publishing, all with the safety of the web business behind me. Thankfully this was the case, as publishing is a much more complicated business financially…

Publishing was fun – and I knew I had arrived at my destination. At the same time I met a beautiful girl at church. She was attractive, smart, savvy and ambitious. However I was shy. Luckily she felt strongly about me, as she positioned herself so that I couldn't not notice her. She lured me in, as I tell people! Or as my Dad used to say, "She chased me until I caught her."

I remember one night I was walking out of church and she was talking to another person. As I walked past her I felt God say to me, "You're going to marry that girl." I calmly got in my car and went home to eat my evening meal. I was so relaxed about it and just knew it would all fall in to place. I don't think she was quite so relaxed about how it would unfold, though!

The day my world became *Alive*

Nicole and I got married the following year in December of 2002. She was working at the same church we both attended and by this time was working as a graphic designer. I had resurrected the events business, plus doing some direct marketing, although not on the same scale as previously, so we were running four companies simultaneously. But there was a fifth company to come... One Saturday afternoon we went up to the church to use her design computer, as Nic was going to design up a couple of entry forms for me. While she was designing away, above her desk was shelving, with the different magazines stored away where the church had advertised.

I pulled out a magazine called *Alive*, which was at the time the major non-denominational magazine in Australia. Prior to this it was called *On-Being*. As I flicked through its pages, I was quite impressed with the way it was laid out. As a publisher, I immediately thought of the ways that I would alter it if I owned it. About a week later we were taking our new Labrador for a walk – the same dog we still had until recently - and as we were walking and talking, Nic mentioned that *Alive* was closing its doors. That was major news, I thought, and immediately the thought went through my mind that maybe this is something I could, or should, get involved in. I wrestled with it all night, and eventually got up quite early to walk and pray about it. As I did I felt God prompting me to write to the current publisher. So I did. Showing how long ago this was, I typed and mailed him a letter. Who does that these days?

The day he got the letter he gave me a call. He was certainly interested and said that if I was serious, then it would be best if we met in person. So I hopped on a plane to Melbourne the next morning. By the end of the day *Alive* was mine. This was exciting, yet surreal, all at the same time. Here I was as the publisher of a prestigious Christian magazine, and although I'd been a Christian pretty much my entire life, I knew nothing about the Christian marketplace. I also had no desire to leave behind the different businesses we were running to move into Christian media. I wasn't prepared to get overly involved in the day-to-day, but I was excited about running the business side of it. This was not my calling, but I was delighted to be able to do this as a ministry business. That had always been one of my goals.

Considering this, Nic resigned from her role in the church and five months into our marriage we started working together. Incidentally, to this day we have only ever worked together. I'm the head, but she is certainly the neck! She tells the head where it should go... So off we started with our fifth business, Christian media. It was a bit of a bumpy start, but somehow we knew God was with us and that He would guide us.

There was a lot of pressure on us from the get go though, as *Alive* had a very strong name and reputation, and as this was not a start up, there were a lot of eyes watching what the new publisher was going to do. By the time we took ownership, it was 30 years old. Boy, did we made some mistakes. I'll share one 'doozy' with you shortly; one that hurt us very badly. We were tracking along quite well with this business, but the thing I started noticing was the lack of synergy. I had an advertising manager in our other publishing company, and so he came on board to sell on *Alive* also. While he was not a Christian, he was a wonderful guy, and this was a chance for him to get more exposure to God.

Christian Woman magazine

Michael would work hard to get the sales for *Alive*, but there was nothing else to sell our clients into. Media works best when there is synergy and that's why most prominent media companies own a wide range of brands. The company that we acquired *Alive* from, 36 Media, also owned another magazine called *Christian Woman*. *Christian Woman* was 50 years old and was a pretty profitable magazine. By this stage I just knew we needed *Christian Woman* alongside *Alive* to make the investment in Christian media worthwhile. Some good friends of ours from church, Chris and Veronica, were over for dinner one night when I started to share this with them. They were in business and so were very switched on. As we discussed it Chris straight out said to us, "Why don't you just ask them if they want to sell it?"

I remember replying saying, "We cannot do this. I think we took a piece of their heart when we took over *Alive*. I don't think we can take the rest of it by taking *Christian Woman* as well."

Over the next few weeks I was praying about this a lot. One day on my early morning prayer walks before work, I remember the Lord saying, "Okay, now is the time to write to the publisher."

So as I started work that morning, I opened my laptop and was ready to email him. Six to eight months had gone by so this time it was time to email, not snail mail. As my emails downloaded and I contemplated what I would say to him on that email, I could barely believe it. There was an email from him, asking me if I was interested in purchasing *Christian Woman*. God was at work again and I was blown away. As I now had a relationship with him, I picked up the phone and gave him a call. Yes, *Christian Woman* was for sale, but there was a catch. There was another party that wanted to acquire it.

It was Tuesday morning and he said he wanted the sale complete by close of business Friday. Each party was to email him an offer, and essentially, the highest offer by Friday afternoon was the winner. It was a long, stressful week. The other party was from the media world and so they knew what they were doing, but I was determined that if God wanted us in Christian media, then I needed *Christian Woman* as part of our stable of products.

Long story short, we got to the end of Friday and we won the tender. I sweetened the deal late Friday by informing the publisher that I would also pay for the current issue to be printed and mailed, even though he was keeping all the ad revenue. I think that was close to an additional $20,000 expense right there, but we simply were not going to miss out on this magazine. I potentially could have saved us $20k, but I knew that long term, this would be money well spent.

I remember taking the call from the publisher to inform us that we were now the proud owners. We had been invited to a dinner party that evening and the call came through just as we arrived at their house. As I hung up the phone I asked Nic to go in ahead of me. I just had to go and pray to God and thank Him. I needed 10 minutes to collect my thoughts. As I prayed, my excitement wasn't so much to do with winning the tender, but more the fact that I could just so clearly see God's hand at work in our lives. God was calling me into this; I was not pushing my way in. I was relieved that He had the reins and was watching over us.

At this point though I still had no desire to be fulltime in Christian media. As a Christian business owned by my holding company, that was perfect. Nic was there mostly running it, leaving me free to work on the big picture of running the rest of our businesses. I was busy trying to build a conglomerate, one of my deep desires. Then suddenly, over the course of the next few months, things started to change. All of the excitement I had for my other businesses started to wane. I could not explain it. Businesses that would keep me up at night with vision and excitement were now starting to become a chore. My energy was being sapped and I could not figure out what was going on.

At the same time I started to get this deep desire for Christian media. It was inexplicable. I bought copies of American magazines and really analyzed what other Christian publishers were doing. It was our first year wedding anniversary and so we escaped up the coast for a five day getaway. While there I visited a local Christian bookshop, which had a wide range of American magazines. I bought up all I could, and I remember that night, when Nic went off to sleep, I sat in the lounge room and poured over these magazines. I was beginning to see opportunities with each page I turned. I was meant to be on holidays, but this down time was giving me some space in my mind to dream.

This weird phenomena continued. Not too long later there was a guest preacher at our church. Nic and I had been to church that morning and close to the time that the evening church started, I felt to go back alone and just spend some time with God. The preacher started, and as she preached, she said, "There is one person here and I can hear God saying that you just need to do one thing differently." It was like a bolt of lightning hit me. I was that person and I knew what that one thing was.

I was going to stay for the prayer after the service, but as soon as the preaching finished I left. My wife noticed I was home early, and at that, I recounted what had happened. God clearly spoke and that I knew exactly what He was telling me. Within a week or two I remember my business plan was over 40 pages long for this business, and that was that. God had, for the first time in my life, told me exactly what he wanted me to do, and while it was a sacrifice letting go of a lot of other revenue streams, I had this quiet confidence that if we did this well, all our needs would be met.

Immediate leadership

It is hard to explain, other than that it was an anointing, that I could enter a marketplace and confidently feel ready to lead from the front. There were many strong organizations in our market, but probably not in print media. There were strong churches, retailers, colleges, missions, schools, book publishers and distributors, but perhaps not magazine publishers.

Normally you'd enter a market and feel a bit intimidated, especially as I was only 30, but for me, that didn't happen. This also went against my nature as while I am passionate, I'm not pushy. Ordinarily I would have gone in gently, but as soon as we entered this market, an anointing came over me where I was ready to roll up my sleeves and 'own' the publishing segment of it. I think all of the business experience I had from the outside world – both good and bad – just seemed to culminate in making me feel a lot older and more experienced than I in fact was. It was like I had been put on this earth to be in Christian media…

Tough lessons

As previously mentioned, our foray into Christian media was not without its challenges and mistakes. In our early days with *Christian Woman* magazine we received an advertising inquiry from the Christian Science Reading Room. It was taken by our ad manager, and we subsequently published their ad and billed them. I remember thinking that a 'Christian science reading room' must be a place where you read books by Christian authors about science and its effect on our earth.

I was so wrong. The first letter with a cancelled subscription came through, then the next, then the next, and so on. As did the phone calls. Sadly I think we lost thousands of subscribers over this, and six-figures in income. It was a devastating error.

We tried to explain that it was innocent, that we didn't know, but how could we tell our readers that we didn't really know what we were doing, that we were winging this? If they had any idea that we were just a young couple trying our hardest, being led by God, but spiritually way out of our depth, I thought they would have ditched us. Looking back, I should have been honest with them. Had I told them that we were just a young couple, that we had been placed in this position not by choice, that we were simply doing our best to build the Kingdom of God through media and we got caught out, we probably could have salvaged thousands of subscribers. Nevertheless as my son's surfing coach says, "You can't put an old head on young shoulders."

We made other errors with *Alive* too. We thought we'd broaden the reader base by having interviews with Pentecostal leaders like Hillsong's Brian Houston. We were hoping to make the magazine as interesting and far-reaching as possible, but many of our readers were 60 plus (back then!) and were conservative, mainline readers... they did not take our attempts to be more inclusive to the greater Christian church world with kindness. No matter how hard we tried, they continued to cancel their subscriptions. I was too young to figure out just how political the church was when it came to denominations.

I remember the heartbreak at watching all of these subscribers across our two magazines ditching us in droves, but at the same time I knew God would honor our efforts to create Christian media that was not for one group, but for a broader audience. And if we had to go backwards while we transitioned, then we'd be okay. This is where all the experience I had gained in business really started coming to the fore. We were now in a leadership position, but we were able to manage it at a young age, as we had skills and experiences that were well beyond our years.

When it costs you something

Looking back I am most proud of the fact that we were keen and hungry to do God's work. Unfortunately, it did not always pay well so Nic and I continued to run our events company and web company alongside our Christian media company in order to survive.

Not many people will know how hard we worked or what we

personally invested into Christian media. Our events company meant weekend work, so Nic and I would work all week (and into the night) and then while others were sitting in a cafe enjoying a coffee on the weekend, we were getting ready for a triathlon! Some of the start times were 2am in order to get all of the roads closed and set up done for a 7am registration. There we were running like crazy so we could continue funding *Alive* and *Christian Woman* magazine and nobody knew.

So often it's easy to stand back and criticize. Criticizing people who step out of the boat and have a go is in fact one of the easiest things to do. To get out of your safety zone and try something different can be terrifying at times. Standing on the sideline and being cynical of the person out there having a go is unfair.

Having said that, criticism is just part of the cost you will pay as a leader, so you've either got to develop thick skin, or realize that potentially you are in the wrong position within the organization.

As I close this chapter, if you're ever fortunate enough to meet my wife (and I use the word 'fortunate' because she is one special lady), don't ever bring up the subject of our triathlon business in front of her. She has very bad memories of it. All of those early starts... summer weekends out at Penrith in the stinking heat in Sydney's west, and winters spent in Parramatta Park, setting up events in the absolute dead of winter. Trying to move the homeless along so we could set up our registration and all to have to go back to work again for the week in our 'day' jobs... I'm not sure she has forgiven me yet for dragging her into that business!

You grow up the day you have your first real laugh
– at yourself.
ETHOL BARRYMORE

CHAPTER TWELVE

THE NO DEBT STRATEGY

As we narrowed in our focus on Christian media, I started formulating a plan for how we were going to make this happen. If we were going to cut the other businesses, which were the ones providing both the cash flow and profits to diversify, then we were going to have to get very savvy as to how this was going to work. I started to see a very big vision in front of me and I distinctly remember the night I was out praying about our future. As this enormous vision appeared in front of my eyes, I said to the Lord, "God, are you sure it is okay to build a Christian empire?"

I remember clearly God rebuking me. His response was along the lines of, "If the world can have the best of everything, then why does work done in my name need to be small and shabby?" This was actually a life-changing moment for me. I hadn't really thought about it too much, as I went to a big church, where everything was done with excellence. It really wasn't until I was removed from the four walls of that church and into this Christian 'industry' that I really started to notice how much of a cottage industry it was.

So I immediately replied, "Okay God, if we are going to do this, then we are going to do it big. The difference is that it will be done for your glory, and not mine." It was a massive step of faith to put all our eggs in the one basket, as it were, and focus in on what I knew we had been called to. But further to this, I felt God offer me two further 'commands', or foundations, on which this business would be based: not to ask for any money, and not to borrow money. This sounded pretty straight-forward in theory, but trying to build a media company without access to capital is near on impossible. To run a business that is going to idle along does not take much financial investment, but to build a business that has the goal of ramping up globally: now that takes serious cash.

We are all where we are today due to our past experiences – both good and bad. I should point out that by now I was pretty beaten. I'd taken some massive knocks in business, and while I had this inner desire to keep pressing forward toward my dream, I was also needing a 'God way' of doing it.

Don't ask for money

Most Christian organizations are non-profits. That doesn't mean they are not intended to make a profit, but rather that their business plan is not centered around making money. Take churches and charities, or missions, as they are called in our market. Without the giving of their members or donors, their operations would not exist, so God was asking me not to ask for money, which meant I was not able to be a non-profit.

There are not a lot of for profit Christian organizations out there, and we were one of them. So this in itself was unusual. However, it meant that we had to come up with commercial ways of funding our business, which I was more than okay with. Churches and charities need donors, but a media company, in my opinion, shouldn't. It should be able to come up with enough income streams if it is savvy enough to fund its operations.

Don't borrow money

The second 'command', or instruction, was not to borrow money. Again, easier said than done. So how were we to build an empire without funding? I put this to God and his answer was simply, "Stick close to me and I will give you the strategies." Great, thanks God... And that has been the story of my life for the last 15 years. By spending that time in prayer and reading God's Word, He has continually brought me fresh ideas, as well as divine connections. I also happen to be married to a very smart, savvy business woman, and no matter what idea I put in front of her, her wisdom has been able to help me decipher between the good ones and the not so good.

While it can be frustrating not having her agree with all of my ideas, at the same time we make a great partnership. Together we discuss every idea. Sometimes I move ahead when she hasn't agreed, and sometimes I have been right. However, many times she has been against an idea, yet I have moved forward regardless, which has left her saying, "I told you so." So her wisdom and support has been priceless. She also has an amazingly strong stomach, or level of faith, and she can handle pressurized situations that a lot of other women would fall apart in. We would not be where we are without her emotional stability and ability to suck up enormous financial pressure. She is way stronger than me in this area.

Not only have we resisted the urge to go to the bank at times, but I have had different Christian business people approach me over the years either wanting to invest in our business, or let me know that they have finance available, should we need it. Again, it has been tempting, but we have said no. I have previously referenced Deuteronomy 28:12, but it is one of the key scriptures I live by:

"You shall lend to many nations, but borrow from none."

Again, I don't think it is wrong or right for Christians to borrow money. Each person needs to make their own financial decisions, but for me, this felt like part of my calling. It also felt like a challenge that I set to God: "Okay God, you're telling me not to ask for money, nor to borrow it. So let's do this. Let's see if this is in fact possible."

To date we have personally invested an enormous amount into our company in in terms of both wages that we haven't taken, as well as 'sweat equity'. We have each literally done the work of several people to keep our costs down and to avoid needing an overdraft for managing paying others. God never told us it would be easy, so we were never under any false illusions as to the challenge in front of us. All we knew was that if we were willing to do His work, then He would be with us and would supply our needs.

Happiness is not a reward – it is a consequence.
Suffering is not a punishment – it is a result.
ROBERT G. INGERSOLL

CHAPTER THIRTEEN

FINDING SYNERGY

Now we had two magazines in our stable, this was just the beginning. As I mentioned, I've always dreamt of having a conglomerate, and as such I knew that this humble beginning was just, well, the beginning. The next thing we started to learn very quickly was that the advertising market was not that big in our 'industry'. So with unsold ad space in each issue, we had to diversify to fill the pages and try and help fund these magazines.

As a publisher you have fixed costs. The cost of printing and mailing that magazine is fixed, as is the cost of office rent, wages and so on, so the more advertising revenue, the better. If you are struggling with ad revenue, then owning other businesses that can be advertised inside your publications is a very worthwhile and sound business strategy. In fact, I used to look at all the major magazines back in the day and wonder why the publishers didn't diversify themselves. They diversified insofar as they owned many media titles, but they weren't in different businesses. Funnily enough, as digital media has taken a bite into advertising, newsstand sales and subscriptions, this is the new strategy all publishers adopt. Media companies will probably be the biggest direct selling companies in years to come.

Ark House Press

Our first diversified business was Ark House Press. I've always loved books, and still do, and so this was a natural fit for us. Did I mention that we literally didn't know the first thing about publishing books? While I have said that the Christian marketplace – at least in Australia and New Zealand – is very cottage industry in the way it as run, there were a few exceptions. Koorong was the major Christian retailer of the day. With 18 stores across the country and a thriving mail order business, they were a very big deal and also very well run. Book publishing was a good fit, just off the back of the sheer number of Christian retailers we had.

We needed someone to run this business so we brought on a very intelligent woman. Emily Francis was screening the manuscripts that were coming in, handling editing and managing the publishing process. Nicole decided on the name 'Ark House' (I cannot take the credit for the name. It was definitely her idea.) and we thought we would test the water with an ad in the next issue of one of our magazines.

We ran a basic quarter-page 'new publishing house looking for authors' ad, and that was the start. We ran the ad in the January/February edition of *Christian Woman*, as that was traditionally a quiet issue in ad sales for us. One basic ad launched one of the major components of our business. I remember coming down with a serious migraine the day before Emily started. I now had a staff member looking to me for guidance, yet I didn't know what I was doing myself.

We started to receive inquiries and it snowballed from there. Just before Emily started, I went out to Koorong's head office to have a meeting with their head book buyers over coffee in their in-store café. I presented her with book one and at the same time shared the vision for what we wanted to achieve. By the time I got back to the office we had a substantial order for the first title. That didn't seem like that big a deal, but given this was nothing more than an idea, I knew that very day that we were on to something. We've since published hundreds and hundreds of titles. We've won the *Christian Book of the Year* awards, we have had authors on TV and radio, both nationally and internationally, and I think we have helped to change the lives of many authors. We also own our own publicity company now and this has become an enormously successful way for authors to get global exposure.

The Christian Business Directory

Hillsong Church had started a business directory called 'The Hillsong Christian Business Directory' and with the size of their church, it was a massive success. I immediately knew that business directories were also a huge opportunity for us. We were knee deep in ad sales, but by this time very proficient in magazine publishing, and a directory was much easier to publish than a magazine. Directories are nothing more than a magazine full of ads... Magazine publishing is a very delicate balance between ad placement and editorial. The balance has to be just right and the ads need to flow through the magazine so that they do not appear obtrusive to the reader, all the while getting the results the advertiser needs. As publisher you need to keep both parties happy. Certainly that was not the case with business directories.

I started to pray to God, as I knew just how many Christian-owned businesses there would be across the country. More than that, I've always believed that Christians should try and support each other, if and when possible. Coming from a Jewish descent (not that anyone in our family is a practicing Jew), I love the way that the Jewish community work together. Almost exclusively. Jews don't share their business with anyone, other than other Jews. They know how to support each other. They can create their own economy and community, and I think that is really special. Anyway, that is another discussion for another time, suffice to say that it is something tht I am passionate about as Initiate Media continues to diversify…

Accordingly my other vision was to use the directories to really create that Christian business community. Before I move on, I will make one more point. The key reason I see Christians in business not able to work together is offense. It is everywhere and it is the scourge of our market and churches. Jews expect things to be done well. They do business together, but if they're not happy with the product or service, then they will really speak up. They won't stand for inferior quality. But if a Christian questioned the quality of another Christian's work, potentially offending that person, apparently that is not okay. So I'll move right along by saying that we need to toughen up, and if we are going to be 'Christians in business', then we need to be downright good at what we do. Lesson over, class dismissed.

I began to pray about this directory, as I knew the revenue would really help us. Hillsong was only operating their directory in Sydney, but there was scope to have a directory in every city in Australia, not to mention other countries. One Friday night good friends of ours, Ross and Karen, came over for dinner. They lived in the inner city and went to Hillsong's City campus. The Directory was actually published by Hillsong's charity arm, Hillsong Emerge. The profits from each Directory were then poured back into charitable community work. Emerge was run out of a separate office in Redfern, which is a short distance from the Sydney city. Due to this proximity to Hillsong City, this is where the Emerge team all went to church.

Ross got to know one of the guys really well, who mentioned to him in passing that Emerge were looking to move on from the Directory. While over for dinner that night he asked me if I would be interested. Would I? This was another God moment. Knowing Ross and Karen really well (we actually introduced them to each other), I couldn't hide my enthusiasm from them. I let Ross know just how keen I was and that I had in fact been praying about this very product for some time. We needed to get our hands on this. It was hard to believe we were even having this conversation.

Ross passed my thoughts on to his contact, who shared them with Emerge's CEO. It was not long before I was invited to a meeting with Leigh and his team to discuss my intensions, as well as theirs. Essentially the main reason they were wanting to move on was because of the potential conflict that the church could be caught up in if there were issues with people doing business together. What if someone paid a builder to do work that was never completed? What if a financial planner invested in the wrong products and saw a family lose all they had? The risks were massive for them. But under our ownership, where we were an independent media company that doesn't face that same emotional risk, it was a perfect fit.

Hillsong was by now starting to get a lot of secular media attention, sadly none of it good, and so their reputation was on the line. It would only take one issue that they had nothing to do with and they could be inadvertently dragged through the mud. It was a series of meetings at Redfern to get this over the line, before one final meeting at their Baulkham Hills head office to sign it off with Hillsong's general manager. Along the way, I got an inside look into the way Hillsong worked and how professional they were. They were not professional to try and be 'corporate' so much as being professional to represent their position in the Christian marketplace as best they could. They were also a massive organization by this stage, so there was a lot of structure around the way they operated.

Hillsong Emerge was at the time based just across the road from the infamous 'Block', an Indigenous housing estate. Think Compton in Los Angeles and you're on the right track. This was a very dangerous place. No-one walked through the Block as I am not sure you would come out alive. One meeting I attended, the CEO had to leave early to attend the Block Christmas party. He walked out the door with the big 'Hillsong' logo emblazoned on his tee-shirt. As he left I asked the others, "Is he safe to walk in there?" To which they replied, "If he is wearing his Hillsong shirt, then he is completely safe."

Hillsong Emerge did so much to support the local Redfern and Aboriginal community that they had huge respect. In fact, at one of the meetings there was a drug deal happening downstairs in their foyer, and as a staff member walked into the meeting room to inform the team, they all immediately jumped up, raced downstairs and went to intercept the deal. They came back to the room pretty quickly though as the moment they got downstairs, the guys saw them and fled. As a guy from the beach, I was not used to heavy scenes like this that occur in the inner city.

As I mentioned earlier, Hillsong was starting to get a lot of media attention. This really ramped up in the years to come and many times I thought to myself, "If the media could see some of the amazing work they actually do, they would let up on them." But of course they didn't, and as the church had such huge annual revenues, they were a pretty easy target. It was interesting to watch though because every time the media slammed them, their churches just continued to grow.

Of course many people believed everything they read, heard or watched, but many others could see straight through the media's tactics and began to support them. Hillsong is pretty much a household name in Australia thanks to all of the free publicity they received. I would dare say if you added up their air time, it would be in the tens and tens of millions of dollars. In fact, it would be a lot more than that.

Directories across Australia and New Zealand

From this acquisition, we launched directories in Melbourne, Adelaide, Perth and South-East Queensland. We then acquired New Zealand's version, known as Christian Contact. This was owned by Elim Church and was a series of six directories across the country. We combined them into one national directory. These were heady days for business directories and unfortunately we probably had one to two good years out of this before print directories started to tank. We had invested six figures in these directory acquisitions so it really hurt when that revenue started to decline. However luckily we had a lot of other things going on, so while it hurt, we were okay. We also more than covered our cost in the profits from the directories we produced.

We have had to sit on the small business side of our organization for quite a number of years, but the outcome of these acquisitions, as well as some work we were doing in America, is that we have ended up with the biggest database of Christian businesses in the world. We have just launched a division called Initiate Business, where we are working really closely with business owners across a range of services. So all things certainly do work together for good, even though it took ten years of sitting on our hands with all of these connections before we could do anything with them again.

Find a Christian

By this stage we had built a really strong seven-figure business. Again it was highly stressful and all-consuming, but at the same time it was really working. We also had *Find a Christian* magazines for schools, colleges and missions, and these were very successfully inserted inside *Alive* and *Christian Woman*. We also launched *Church Today* and *Fundraising Success* magazines. We started moving into the fundraising market as well and with another company joint ventured a big conference called 'The Fundraising Summit'. This was highly successful and brought in a lot of revenue.

Anointed for Business

I was also immensely passionate in my early thirties about helping Christians in business. I remember watering the lawn after work one day when I felt the desire to launch a conference for Christian business people. We did and called it 'Anointed for Business'. We ran it in Sydney, Brisbane and Auckland. We also extended it over to Los Angeles, but in reality we didn't have the connections there just yet, so it didn't get off the ground.

While I was really passionate about this event, it was also probably at the wrong time of my life. I still had very young children so had literally no spare time. I was also still grappling in the back of my mind that I was a surfer, not some businessman who could be fronting a business conference. I had a massive vision for running conferences for Christians in business, but it was the wrong timing. I had too much to achieve still before I would feel comfortable being at the head of such an event, and being 32 years-old at the time, I was just not ready.

I really squirmed sitting on that front row. At the start of each conference, as well as in between speakers, then at the conclusion of the event, I was the 'face'. I've always looked a little younger for my age, so I probably looked like a twenty-something standing up there. While business was motoring along and we were doing really well, in the back of my mind I had an enemy constantly accusing me that I was in no position to be a business leader. Where was my degree? Where was my MBA? With my upbringing shouldn't I just be a lifeguard or swim coach? A global business was no person for a guy like me... I ran these conferences for two years and then stopped. Thankfully some guys from Melbourne started up an event called 'Cre8' and took over, which was a relief, as I didn't want to leave the marketplace without an event. Interestingly, we are re-entering this market again with a new event called 'Inspired Business Live'...

By this stage we also had two young children. I was working from home much of the time as Nic, our art and marketing director then (and now), really had to be in the office to coordinate all of the books, magazines, supplements and client services work that was going on. It wasn't until our third child, Hayden, went to school that Nicole and I both really became fulltime in the company. I used to joke that we had built a seven-figure organization from the ground up, and I was only doing it part-time. The fact that God was in the centre of our business was just so apparent.

The pain of growth
Another successful start up, which is still a major part of our business to this day, was the launch of Initiate Agency. Because we were fairly cutting edge with our design, which really made the difference for our company, we saw the opportunity to be an agency for other organizations as well. We were already working as an advertising agency in that we were doing a lot of creative work for clients. We were designing lots of ads, which would lead to brochures, re-branding and so on. So we decided to make it official by calling our advertising agency Initiate Agency.

It was a fairly natural decision and so we were pretty busy early on. We also started to do a lot of work for an agency in the city. They had an office full of people and were winning a lot of work, and we were back-ending this for them. I was more than happy to do this as the extra income was very handy. We were flat out working with them when I started to notice the age of some of their invoices. They were getting older and older, and I started to worry that something was up. It was. They had run out of cash and gone into liquidation, owing us a lot of money. We didn't see a cent of it. The owner apologized and then promptly set up a new business just down the road, taking all his new work elsewhere. I don't think our unpaid bills worried him at all. We got through it though and that is where our diversity has always been a Godsend for us. We have always had multiple income streams and the Grace of God to get through!

I saw agency work as a really big opportunity for us. A guy in our church at the time was running a very successful ad agency with some very big multi-national clients. He suggested we acquire his company. If we were to do this it would give us access to some amazing creative talent, but at a pretty high cost as well. With each meeting I didn't feel right about it, and in the end we did not proceed. They were carrying quite a lot of debt, and although their acquisition would have added a couple of million dollars to our revenues, Nic and I didn't need that extra pressure. We were instead happy to bide our time and build this part of our business organically.

Interestingly the day we brought on a new Business Development Manager to really ramp up Initiate Agency, I was struck down by another mind-numbing migraine. We met at the office and I took our new staff member up the road for a coffee, just to make it a warm start to our company. We headed back to the office to start getting stuck in to all that needed to be done, as well as the systems and software she had to learn, when this migraine came on. I had to give her the day off and I took off out the door to get to bed, popping my migraine pills as I left. I only share this because it really does show the extent of pressure I was facing in building and stretching out. While vision and dreaming was a natural place for me and brought great strength, the financial side didn't. All the responsibility I was carrying was a massive weight on my shoulders and so I was paying a high price for this fast business growth. Our weekly outgoings were massive and so while we were highly successful for a young couple, it was coming at a high price for me. During this time in my life I was so stressed that I barely surfed. Business was all consuming and so I had no energy for much else. I retreated into my shell a little, as by the weekend I was mentionally and emotionally exhausted from keeping the organization not only moving forward, but all the expenses paid.

No man ever made a great discovery without the exercise of the imagination.
GEORGE HENRY LEWES

CHAPTER FOURTEEN

COUNTING THE COST

Migraines have been a major concern for me, brought on by the stress of business. My first one occurred while I was doing that chicken roll early morning delivery job. A group of guys and girls from my church went to the snow for the weekend. I remember climbing into bed at 12.45am and my alarm going off at about 4.30am. I'd had less than four hours sleep before I got to the factory and as I walked into the cool room to pack the van, this violent flashing started appearing across my eyes. I had no idea what it was.

I set out on the road and within five minutes I could barely see where I was going. For those non-migraine sufferers, one of the scariest parts of the onset of a migration is the flashing, or the loss of vision, as it is a sign of what is coming. I get both. If that is not bad enough, then the next part is by far the worst. Around the 20-minute mark the pain starts to kick in. For me, it is a four-hour process where it literally feels like my head is in a vice that has been tightened way too tight over my forehead, yet I cannot do anything about it. It hits me just above the right eye and feels like someone is trying to extract my eye while I am lying there.

As I had never had a migraine before, I naturally had no pain relief. That morning was probably one of the worst experiences of my life. From 5am to 9am, I have never been through anything like it. I am not even exaggerating when I say that I could have driven that van into oncoming traffic, just to escape the pain. Suicide was literally an option that morning.

Sadly, that was the first of many to come. From my mid-twenties onwards, my life has been marred by them. In fact, until my mid-thirties, they literally controlled my life. I would not go anywhere that was not a pretty quick drive home so I could get to bed. Or at worst, I'd make sure that there was a bed nearby where we were going so I could pop my pills and climb on in.

I went to see my doctor and he prescribed me with special sleeping pills. They were so powerful that if I was traveling overseas, then I had to carry a note from my doctor to prove he prescribed them. Security could have mistaken me for a drug addict otherwise.

I'd barely go to a meeting in the city. I flat out would not fly. The pain of each migraine was so intense that if I happened to pop two pills with the onset of a migraine, then I could not drive, I could not walk, I couldn't even talk. The upside was that if I could get them in my bloodstream immediately, then I'd be so knocked out that I could sleep right through the pain. However, if I was on the road and there was no chance to sleep, then I couldn't take the pills. That was when I would be a zombie for four hours, and taking my life during a couple of migraines honestly crossed my mind so I could relieve myself of that pain.

I remember when they were becoming a regular occurance I had a meeting in the city. I was so sick of migraines controlling my life that I was determined to fight through. So I kept the appointment and left for the trip regardless. It was a terrible idea. The two substitute tablets known as Paracetamol did absolutely nothing to help and I literally sat in that meeting, unable to recall anything that was said. Not to mention the one hour round trip.

Another time I had a client from Melbourne who wanted to spend the day with our team getting her company's website finalized. I don't know why, but I agreed to collect her from Sydney Airport, before transporting her to our office we had at the time in North Sydney. Ernie and his team of developers were based about a half mile down the road in the suburb of Milsons Point and had not yet arrived for work, so we sat in the boardroom in North Sydney before going to Milsons Point and started going through the specs. As we sat there that violent flashing started. I didn't know what to do. I had this client in my trust until 6pm that evening, and it was only about 8am. This was bad.

Not only could I not tell her what was happening, but I also could not take any medication. My special meds would have seen me just lay on the floor and go to sleep. If I could somehow get through the next 4 hours, I'd be okay. It was as bad as expected, and luckily down in Milsons Point Ernie did all the talking, so I could sit back a little and focus on myself. I finally got home at about 7.30pm and just collapsed. Another time I had three migraines back to back and was in bed for a full 48 hours.

If I was going to be able to go to certain meetings, which I had to if I was to have any income, then I had to do something about it. I worked out a plan. I knew where the hotels were around the city, and that way if I couldn't get to my bed, I'd not be too far away from hopping into someone else's. I had about twenty minutes from the time I could feel a migraine coming on to being so delirious that I couldn't speak. That was enough time to get to get to the hotel, do a quick check-in, and get into bed. I learned one skill from it though: because I only traveled to the super important meetings, I learned to work with people from a distance. I could 'meet' people all over the world with Skype and my phone. Now we have people in different locations, I'm more than comfortable to meet with them – without having to be face to face. I cannot tell you how much money we have saved on business travel! In fact I nearly missed out taking on *Alive* as I was nearly not going to fly to Melbourne for the day.

There is one upside to getting older as a migraine sufferer, and that is that migraines do taper off in intensity. Those monthly migraines, where I was knocked out for a day and then needed the second day to recover, were now not so bad. In fact, the last year has seen me drop carrying migraine medication. I keep some Asprin with me at all times, but I can now get by with Asprin and an ibuprofen. I had my last migraine a week ago from the day I write this, and I think I have had about four in the last three years. I feel like I have my life back!

Another upside is that I really learnt to look after myself from a young age. I had to get good sleep, had to be well hydrated at all times, and I had to have a good diet. These three things are essential for the migraine sufferer. I refused to give up coffee though…

I share this with you not to whinge or complain about the challenges I have faced, but because there can be a real cost to what you're wanting to achieve. I know that God is with us, but at the same time the bills don't get paid just by miracles. We, like everyone else in business, have walked down some terrifying paths. The real difference has been in having our Creator there to offer support.

However, it's important to remember that what is sown in tears is reaped in laughter. Starting a business is tough, but there is always a season – at some point – where you will reap all of your hard work. You just have to be very patient...

Many men owe the grandeur of their lives
to their tremendous difficulties.
CHARLES H. SPURGEON

CHAPTER FIFTEEN

WHEN PUBLISHING HIT THE WALL

We were so far out on the edge in trusting God that it was not funny. Sometimes I think maybe too far. We were zooming along, and while I could see the Internet could change our business, with part-time work (as I was hardly in the office, looking after young children at home so Nic could oversee all the jobs going to the printers), I literally didn't have a spare moment to work on the transition to digital. Interestingly enough I had all the skills though, so it wasn't a role that I had to palm off to someone else to do.

When we broke for our 2008 Christmas Party, life was good. Business was always hard and cash flow was constantly tight, but things were going really well. We organized a big lunch at our home and had it fully catered for. Prior to the lunch though, we had all the team at the office for a vision morning. Different staff members flew in for the day and it was a great occasion. I stood before our team and told them what a great year we had, how well it was all going, and how big our plans were for the future. We all broke from the meeting in a jovial mood and made the twenty-minute drive to our home for a beautifully catered lunch. When all the team left, I distinctly remember driving to collect the children from pre-school for the last day of the year feeling so good about the day, the year, the Christmas break I desperately needed, and then how good the year ahead was going to be.

The office door closed that afternoon for the summer break and we all deserved a good rest. Indeed you can tell this was pre-Internet, as no one's office closes anymore! The Internet never sleeps. One of the announcements I was able to make that morning was that we had reached an agreement to acquire *DayStar* magazine in New Zealand. I had just returned from NZ a couple of weeks before Christmas to negotiate the deal. *DayStar* was the New Zealand equivalent of Australia's *Alive*, so this was a major deal. This was going to open many doors into NZ, which was beyond exciting for me.

Hitting the wall

I broke for Christmas and really enjoyed the break, knowing there was lots of exciting projects to go back to work to. As we headed back at the start of January, it was strangely quiet. The Global Financial Crisis had hit the year before, but it never seemed to get near us. The first week was quiet, then the next, then the next. I remember being on the phone to Nic one day in late January and telling her I was really starting to get worried. Advertisers were pulling back, orders weren't coming in, and in the space of a few weeks we had lost all momentum. All of this was aside from the fact that January is traditionally a quieter month.

By the very start of February I was due to fly to New Zealand to sign the paperwork on *DayStar*. The thought had crossed my mind that maybe it was time to pull out, but I guess a combination of my pride and perhaps a little too much faith meant I flew over and signed it regardless. So not only were we slowing in Australia, but now we had full responsibility for another monthly magazine in NZ, along with a few staff that made the transition with us.

DayStar started tanking quickly. While other areas were hurting us, no one was really noticing or watching on, but with this publication, we had a board of five Directors who signed off on the deal, as well as new staff, and from the get go we were sinking. It was only a few months later that I had to call one of the Directors and tell him we were badly struggling and were going to have to move the magazine from monthly to bi-monthly, as the advertising sales were slow (yet the print and staffing bills weren't).

This was probably one of the most embarrassing and humbling periods of my life. In hindsight they would have faced the same issues as I did, but as it was now under my ownership. Unfortunately, history shows that *we*, not them, forced it to close. The magazine was controlled by a great group of Directors who really had their hearts in the right place in publishing *DayStar*. They were smart people too, and so they didn't let it move into our stable with ease. Luckily they were fair-minded and no one gave me a hard time. By this time the agreement was signed anyway, so they couldn't do anything about it. However one of their greatest concerns was that I was buying *DayStar* so I could put it out of business and then turn *Alive* into an Australian and New Zealand publication. I gave them assurances that this was not the case, but I think it looked like that was exactly what I was trying to do.

Moving to digital

At this time there was a lot of talk that magazines would move to digital. Ad sales were dropping, but one of the biggest factors was that while publishers were bleeding from the GFC, paper prices not only rose, but the post office was putting up their mailing rates. So while publishers were doing their very best to get through, they were being hit from all sides. The iPad had hit the scene and there was talk that Steve Jobs's latest invention would re-invent magazines in a similar way to what the iPod did with music.

We moved a number of magazines to digital, but the advertisers were never really interested. They liked to be able to see the magazine on their desk, view their ad, and feel satisfied with their ad spend. We were definitely very early to the digital magazine table, but we really had no other choice. I knew digital was the future for print media, but the market was some years away from feeling the same.

By this time we were still getting hammered, and as a result, it was time to let staff go. This was the toughest thing to do. We were a team of 20 at this point, so we had to trim down. Not only was it hard on those going, but it created a lot of uncertainty for those staying. Naturally the mood in the office changed pretty quickly and I literally dreaded going in to work each day. I felt like I had gone from the visionary CEO to the exact opposite.

The reality is that I had no other option. I would get my coffee from my local coffee shop and some days I could barely bring myself to get in the car and drive to the office. I just couldn't face another day. It was hard enough having to re-structure our business model and deal with a cash crisis, let alone having to do it while letting people go.

I clearly remember having to inform one particular staff member that I was making her position redundant. I thought I'd take her for a coffee at the shopping centre up the road to soften the news I was about to give her. They had one key coffee shop that was the go-to for all the coffee buffs, and as we sat there that morning and exchanged pleasantries, I got down to the reason we were meeting. As I informed her she was losing her job, she burst into tears and started howling in front of all the patrons. It was mostly Mums and children in there, so for all they knew we might have been a married couple and I was asking her for a divorce. I told her to just take the day off so she could deal with this, and she jumped up and quickly exited. I sat there, all eyes on me, and quickly got up and left.

Looking back, I should have let those staff members go much earlier. We carried them for so long that Nic and I personally suffered the ramifications for quite a few years to come.

By this time I was at my wits end, (and I thought the direct marketing pain was bad). This was another level. I now had a wife, two children – with a third on the way – as well as an expensive office to run. We also had staff in two countries to support. We had upgraded to a much bigger (and naturally more expensive) home. Cutting the costs and re-shaping this business was going to come with a lot of pain. I remember one night going for a long walk literally asking God why He had forsaken me. I was having my own Job experience. What had I done that was this bad that I deserved this? The pain was really that bad, and the situation was getting dire. I believe that, aside from prayer, the one thing that got us through this was humility. I have always been a reluctant businessman, and as such I knew my success to date was based on God, and God alone. While I knew I had a knack for it, the business world per-se has never interested me (and it still doesn't). I love business and working hard, but I'm also a bit of a business rebel at heart. I'm not into the business scene. Give me my surfboard and time with my family any day.

God's blessing and humor in the storm
In the middle of this year we were due to have our third child. What should have been a really exciting time was exactly the opposite. The day he was born I just knew he was coming. I woke up that morning and informed Nic I wasn't going to go to the office. But the clincher came when I said, 'I'm going to the café to get a coffee. Would you like one?" When she replied in the negative I just knew that today was the day. She was having minor contractions during the day and so it was a long day at home, just working quietly. My Mum and sister were ready and waiting for our call to come down to take the other two children for us so we could head to the hospital. They were only two and four years-old, so not yet at school. As she kept up the mild contractions for most of the day, I rang them and asked them to meet us at the hospital, as we could not work out when we would be leaving.

By about 3pm in the afternoon Nic knew it was time to go.

We were all packed and I told the little ones that we needed to be ready at a moment's notice. As I was getting the kids into the car I saw Nic go into the lounge room, get down on her knees and go through a pretty big contraction. By now I was nervous. Having been there twice before, I knew this was not an early contraction. She was well into labor.

We hit the road and the car was quiet. Nic was already starting to look pale. We were a 45-minute drive to the hospital, so I knew we were in trouble. By now school was out and there was a lot of traffic on the road. Sydney is a big, busy city, and if you catch her at peak hour, she is very unforgiving. Why didn't we leave earlier? I'm glad you asked. Because Nic's contractions were changing throughout the day, the hospital were super busy and they told us that if we came early and she was not ready, then they would simply send us home. With a 90 minute round trip we were not prepared to drive there, only to drive home again.

We got to the top of a long road called the Wakehurst Parkway and Nic let out an almighty roar. By this point I knew the baby was coming. About 500 meters down the road she undid her seatbelt. I started getting hot; that heat that comes on you when major stress occurs. We were still a good twenty-minutes from the hospital, and she was well and truly ready. She let out an almighty howl, then started to push. I was driving down the Warringah Freeway in the inside lane, trying to get to hospital as quickly as I could, when I looked over and saw our little boy's head. There was a gas station at the bottom of that stretch of road, which I promptly pulled into. By the time I steered the car into one of their parking spots, my wife was holding little

Hayden in her arms.

It was so overwhelming that I was trying to turn off the car, but I couldn't. The car was still in the drive position, but I was so stressed that I couldn't bring it up to the park position. I finally came to my senses, raced to the boot of the car, where Nic had luckily packed a blanket, given it was winter, and we wrapped our little baby in it. The whole family was in the car and on hand to welcome him. We called the ambulance, got to the hospital, and the rest, as they say, is history. I tell this story because it shows that in the worst year in our lives, God not only had a little gift for us, but he had a sense of humor, too. This event brought so much joy and laughter in the midst of so much struggle. Deep down, we knew God had our backs, but there was still a lot of fighting left to do.

God's tomorrow will be better
than any yesterday you have ever known.
THOMAS A. CARRUTH

CHAPTER SIXTEEN

I NEED A BREAKTHROUGH

I was spending many hours a night pounding the pavement, seeking God for direction. My trusty Labrador (who loved a really long walk) joined me on those silent night time walks, marking the trees as he trotted along, leaving me to seek God without distraction.

I just couldn't get a vision and I badly needed one, but I kept turning up, pleading with God to show me the way. Then one night it happened. As I walked, this fresh digital vision just flashed before my eyes. It was so clear and so concise that for the first time in many months, I saw fresh opportunity. It was such a strong God vision that I wrapped up the walk quickly and raced home to chat to Nic.

Now this little piece of information here will show you how badly we needed direction. With three young children (three of them under four years of age) getting them down to bed was a minor miracle. By the time we got through bathing, dinner, reading and finally getting them off to sleep, we were literally spent. Nic's one show that she loved to watch each night was on. Even she would admit that it was average at best, but having it on was her signal that the day was over and she could put her feet up and just relax.

I came rushing through the door and said, "We have to talk." Now the seriousness of the moment, and how badly we "had to talk" was that I pulled up my laptop and we started making notes. I saved this particular document at 7.20pm, which might not mean much to you, but this was smack in the middle of her show. Nic is one of the hardest workers I know, but she also has clear boundaries. After 6pm at night, work is over and she is happy to wait and pick it up again in the morning. We are quite different like that! If we did need to discuss business after hours, we would at least wait until she had caught her breath, had a bit of time out, and had the headspace for a deep conversation.

So to give up that valued breather at the end of the day to discuss business meant it was really important. Nic is always slower to come on board with ideas than I am. She is quite reserved and calculated, and that's why we are such a good team. She is calm and collected and will look at the positive and negatives, where I am a 'glass half full' kind of guy. So for her to turn off the TV and then immediately buy in as I started sharing the vision, I knew that it was the right move!

A new direction

That vision God had showed me this night was incredible. I saw an online news portal that meant no magazine printing, which in turn meant no more massive print bills or distribution woes.

Print magazines are exceptionally expensive to distribute and thus running multiple titles is a fairly stressful business. A digital centric business would allow us to reach more people than we ever could from our small Australia and New Zealand market. This new direction would be nothing like the Christian market had seen and we were attempting it.

In fact, the vision was much more than just providing content. The business model was naturally based around content, as we are a media company, but it was so much more. I envisaged us branching out into a wide array of businesses. With media as the first connection point, I saw us building a massive network of businesses that complement each other, while at the same time benefitting Christians globally. I had run so many businesses and had so much experience that I was confident that I could turn my hand to other businesses that would not only appeal to Christians on a global basis, but would allow the Christian marketplace to create its own ecosystem of sorts. Going back to the way the Jewish do business, to this day I firmly believe we can do the same thing for the Christian marketplace.

So with this new vision burning, while the pain of making the transition had not gone, we had renwed energy, which took away much of the sting. I have always told God that I was doing this for Him, and that I was prepared to walk away at any moment. Right when I was ready to, and was already looking at different industries, He showed His hand and gave us fresh vision.

Even with a new vision and direction, it was a stressful period. Our financial position had not changed and we still had some cleaning up (financially speaking) to do. Transitioning to digital media meant design and development costs on top of lower revenue. Having had a web development company previously was now a tool in my business belt. I knew how the process worked and I had some great developers on hand to help bring this vision to pass. We were so fortunate that we were young enough to embrace this new digital age without it seeming like a foreign language. As I have said to my wife on many occasions, we're old enough to have the business skills to lead this new frontier, but young enough to really understand this new world, and thankfully, I was once more knee deep in high-end web development. We wouldn't be where we are today if it was not for that web business. We wouldn't have had the capital to build the websites we have without hiring in the talent to do it.

The publishing world was run by older executives, and transitioning to digital was both complex and expensive to do. They were very experienced men and women, but the reality for the smaller companies was that they did not have the skillset – nor the capital to employ the right digital experts – to transform digitally. Many up and retired, many went under, and many people, who had worked hard their entire lives, watched all they had worked for dissipate.

It was a sad time for many in publishing, advertising and retail. It's probably very hard to make such a massive transition when you're in those later years. You know your business so well, but you just don't have the energy to go through a revolution. The really big publishers were once again the big winners, as they had the money to pay the best in digital to come in and transform their businesses into part print, part digital.

On a smaller scale we were also fortunate to be print publishers as well. The pure play Internet – or digital – publishers, while they had great ideas, were very short on cash. So while we cleaned up our business and brought our staffing in line with our digital business, we were able to carry digital because of strong print. By 'print' I primarily mean book publishing, but we also kept a few magazines in print too. We have swung back into some magazine and newspaper publishing, but certainly not on the scale of what this formerly was.

So it's a very exciting future and the most exciting part is that we're not just building a business, but we are spreading the Word of God to the ends of the earth.

The need to be in daily news

One thing the Internet and its free news has done is given people of all ages an appetite to know what is going on around them. News was once for the older group who went down to the shops to buy their newspaper, or for the couple that couldn't miss the morning and evening news.

The media served up the news as they saw fit and selected the time that we could watch it. Or the newspaper was printed at 4.00am, so if something tragic happened at 7.00am, you could miss the whole thing. I still remember the day that 9/11 occurred. I was in the web business and had an early meeting in the city with an ad agency that we did all of their web work for and as I drove in, I decided to put on a CD instead of listening to the radio. With no online news or Facebook feeds back then, I had no idea of the tragedy that had unfolded.

This just cannot happen in this day and age. If something happens, we all know about it in real time. As we moved in to publishing, I prided myself on the fact that *Alive* was a cutting edge publication, as it did keep Christians abreast of the news around them (at least on a monthly basis!). As we were moving along and diversifying, a study was done on where Christians got their news from. Predictably we were not even mentioned. So for all the migraines and other pain I suffered to be in media, we weren't even on that radar. Ouch.

Something had to change. I'd always dreamt of having a portal. I'd seen msn.com back in the early days, and now Yahoo was the market leader. Portals allowed you to go to one place and do so much more than just read the article you intended to. Many years before I got a clear vision of having a portal (but not in the Christian market) when I started to carve out the idea for our market. If we could get a high volume of traffic, then we had the business skills to transition that traffic into income streams that we could develop.

myChristiandaily.com

Nic and I sat down one morning to discuss this. I started the conversation with the findings of that study and how, if we were going to influence the world, then we had to have a fast-moving website. She immediately agreed and she came up with the name of 'My Christian Daily' during our meeting. We needed a major news site of our own. This was slightly before some of the new software that is available now, and so we mocked up this big website on Nic's computer, before tendering it out to be built. It was a massive site and an expensive job to build. That's the easy part though. Now you have to staff it so there is constant content… News never sleeps in this Digital Age.

We did a pretty good job with the first version of

mychristiandaily.com, but at the same time it definitely didn't look like the sites that the big news companies had. At this time one of our staff in New Zealand, Ray Curle, gave me a call and said that he had been chatting to a developer who had built a really impressive news website, but he was not interested in then having to fill it with content. A 'techy', it was fun for him to build, but he had no interest in expanding it and putting in the energy necessary to make it a major site. I just happened to know a company that did have the energy to make it work...

I spoke to him the same day and within a few days we had agreed to acquire it. This was massive for us because although we had to find the money to buy it, we also needed a rock solid platform to work from. We now had this, and while we have always been savvy enough to find income streams, at the very heart of our organization's DNA is media. It's great that we build websites and apps, that we publish books and do a myriad of things (did I mention that we have recently acquired an insurance company and we are about to roll out insurance?), but we are after all a media company, and that is at our core.

We were now a news player and able to see our message – as well as influence – spread literally all over the world. In fact recently one of our articles noting that Hillsong's Brian Houston was a supporter of Australia not introducing same-sex marriage had just under 200,000 reads within a short time frame (and the site now has more than 17,000 articles on it). Now that's influence. That is why we spend our lives doing this. Nic and I could be in many other industries that pay a lot more and potentially do not require us to work so hard, but that doesn't interest either of us. We know what we have been put on this earth to do, and so we do it with a joyful heart.

My Christian Daily, while being a long way off driving the key revenue into our company, gives us that influence to present the message of God in a contemporary way. It helps Christians keep informed of what is going on around them, it covers the news that the mainstream outlets will often push to the side, and at the same time it helps keep the torch held high that Christianity and the church is alive and well in the 21st century.

I am a massive believer that Christianity has a very bright future, and I am invested in helping spread the word about the hope to the world. In an era of fake news, or important issues that are being swept under the carpet, I believe we have an important role to play.

I believe Christianity is going to see its best days. I am invested in this. The secular media are working overtime to push God and Christianity to the side. You can barely even hear about Jesus now at Christmas and Easter. Santa and the Easter Bunny have hijacked these sacred events. However, we are going to keep spreading the Word of God to the ends of the earth. Our best days are ahead!

What's next?
Honestly, God only knows. As mentioned, we have just this year acquired an insurance start up, we have completed a joint venture on a great directory product called *Which Christian*. We bought out our joint venture partnership in christianhomeswap.com, meaning we now own 100% of the site. We are also working on a new house sitting site right now. We are launching a new venture with Ark House, where authors keep the rights to their book.

Plus we have a new website called findachristian.co. and we are doing more and more creative work for clients. We are moving into church and small business services... the opportunities are never ending.

In all of this though, I am working on spending a lot more of my time writing and speaking, helping to mentor other people and business owners. I love to delegate and as such I am constantly passing work on to others to ensure that, while Initiate Media continues to be a cutting edge Christian media company, I have the time to write, speak and work with others. This is something I am really passionate about, but balancing my time when I have a very busy company, as well as four young children, will be a challenge time-wise.

Fortune favors the audacious.
DESIDERIUS ERASMUS

CHAPTER SEVENTEEN

FINAL THOUGHTS

Writing this book has been especially painful at times. When I look forward in business, I am filled with faith. I feel like I can achieve anything. We're on the right path, all is well, and so life is faith-filled and there are loads of opportunities up ahead. However, looking back drags up all of the challenges and issues we have faced. Many times I've wanted to stop writing so I could forget about the past, but unfortunately that is not the way life works.

It is our past failures, losses and disappointments which, if handled well, open the doors for new opportunities. In the Bible you will read that God struck Jacob's hip, leaving him with a permanent limp so he would never forget that moment (Genesis 32:22-32). In my life, I feel like God has done the same. The pain is so great in a few areas that when I would ordinarily travel back down that path, the limp in my hip is so evident that I think better of it. It has helped me on many, many occasions. So as you read this story, there is no boasting in writing it. Instead I want to encourage you that if *I* can do it, then so can you.

I am also bringing up the bad as well because it is only fair to you, the reader, that you see both sides. Many times I read biographies and the author will boast about their successes, but gloss over their failings very quickly. I know why they do it, but what happens is the rest of us think we are somehow unusual in that we are taking beatings, while they just seem to go from strength to strength. In fact, I read a book at the start of the year called *Shoe Dog* by Phil Knight, the founder of Nike. This is the most honest biography I have ever read. Phil Knight could have used his book as a 'chest-beating' opportunity and told the world just how great he is (in my eyes he is phenomenal), but instead he gave a raw account of his business life. That honesty has helped changed my life. The pain he went though to build Nike is way beyond anything I have even remotely faced. I think about him often when I am facing challenges.

It's like social media: we are all guilty of just posting the highlights of our lives, but imagine if people sent photos of their overdue notices, their tax bills, their re-possession notices and on and on. We'd all breathe a collective sigh of relief, knowing that we are all walking through challenges. They may be different. Your challenge might be a really difficult child, or a major problem in your marriage when your finances are fine, but they are challenges and stresses nonetheless that we each need to have faith to get through.

What makes greatness is starting something
that lives after you.
RALPH W. SOCKMAN

CHAPTER EIGHTEEN

JOURNEYING TOGETHER

It sounds corny, but I am with you on your journey. The thing that has encouraged me to write this book is that I am in the game too. I'm not the retired athlete, now standing on the sideline as the coach. Back when I was a swim coach I'd set these massive sessions for my swimmers, then I'd pop to the canteen and order a hot chocolate. I felt guilty at times that they were right there in front of me, torturing themselves at times in that pool (some literally vomiting at the end of a torturous set), while I was just to the side, able to have a drink, something to eat, chat to passers by, and so on.

In business, I am still the swimmer in the pool too. I'm in the same squad like you are. I'm not the coach or advisor. I am at times feeling the same pain that you may be. The media world is being tipped upside down and the changes and challenges show no signs of abating. It's actually *NOT Business As Usual* for me, also.

So I champion you to go forward and to accept challenges as

part of your journey. If it were easy, everyone would be doing it. I have nearly given up many times, and barely a month goes by where I don't just double-check with God that He is still with me and that this is what I should be doing. As I mentioned earlier, I am a reluctant businessman. It's by the grace of God that I do what I do. You will find me many days in the week with salt still in my hair, as I have had a surf with my boys before or after work. I am not an atypical businessman, and you don't need to be either to do something exceptional. Just go with your skills and talents, give to God whatever is in your hand, and see where He might take you.

As for me, I am, however, at an age and stage of life where I want to use much of my knowledge to help others. We have a good team, as well as systems in place in our company and as such I am spending more of my time writing and slowly helping others. I'm a long way from the top, but I am also a few rungs further along than some others. Naturally, there are those who are many rungs ahead of me, but my future lies in balancing my time between Initiate Media and writing and speaking.

I hope my story will help you in some small way. I'd even like to stay in contact. If you visit www.mattdanswan.com then you can sign up to my regular newsletter, or you can connect with me on social media. I won't bombard you with anything as I simply don't have the time!

A MILLION DREAMS
THE GREATEST SHOWMAN (2017)
WRITTEN BY Benj Pasek & Justin Paul
SUNG BY Hugh Jackman, Michelle Williams, Ziv Zaifman

Every night I lie in bed
The brightest colours fill my head
A million dreams are keeping me awake
I think of what the world could be
A vision of the one I see
A million dreams is all it's gonna take
A million dreams for the world we're gonna make

However big, however small
Let me be part of it all
Share your dreams with me
You may be right, you may be wrong
But say that you'll bring me along
To the world you see
To the world I close my eyes to see
I close my eyes to see

A Million Dreams lyrics © Sony/ATV Music Publishing LLC, Kobalt Music Publishing Ltd.

THE ENTREPRENEUR'S WIFE

NICOLE DANSWAN

I'm a bit of a creative type with an administrive brain. It seems like an odd combination, but for me, it sums me up fairly accurately. From a young age I would spend hour upon hour dreaming and making up stories. My imagination ran wild and I was often lost in a wonderful world of romance, intrigue and far away places.

My Dad was a journalist. He worked in both magazines and newspapers and as a young child we would often go on some adventure so he could write about it. Growing up with my love of words, I thought I would end up following in his footsteps, however, a move interstate and personal issues saw my focus shift from study to survival. My dreams were well and truly put aside.

After finishing high school, I managed to get a job at a printing company. It was not the dream I had for my life but it would fill time while I tried to work out what I would do as a career path. The pay was terrible and the male staff deplorable, but I met a beautiful girl called Nicole (funnily enough) in the pre-press department. She was blonde (like me) and had beautifully manicured hands. She drove a brand new VW Beetle with a big fake daisy popping out of the dashboard. She was a graphic designer. Her days were filled with colour, shapes and type and I imagined myself in her shoes. What a fantastic job and life she had. She didn't have to run around the factory or make coffee for her peers. Her days were spent creating; turning a blank document into a kaleidescope of colour.

An incredible God-encounter saw my time at the printing company come to an end and I found myself enrolled at the School of Creative Arts in Oxford Falls, Sydney. Under the leadership of Jeff Crabtree (one of my all-time favourite people) and his team, I spent my days studying the Word of God plus dancing full-time. My two years spent there were incredible, but I finished with my Diploma and little direction to what was next.

'I do'

I met Matt at Christian City Church Oxford Falls four children and one Labrador ago (okay, 17 years ago). From the moment we met, everything seemed to align. We shared the same passions, (except for reading material. He was in the middle of four business biographies and I was reading a romance novel, but we both knew that we were 'meant to be'. After a few successful coffee dates after church, he finally plucked up the courage to ask me out on our first date. I was incredibly nervous (and also incredibly sick with the flu), but I was not missing that date for anything or anyone! A limb could have fallen off my body and I still would have gone. That night I mentally checked off my 'future husband must-haves list' (what can I say, I'm an admin kind of girl too - I like lists!) and Matt passed with flying colours.

We were married in December of 2002 and quite honestly we have not looked back since.

At the time of meeting Matt, I was working for the School of Creative Arts (SCA) as the Principal's Personal Assistant. It was a fantastic role and I adored the work, the students and my boss, Jeff Crabtree. Meeting Matt in the midst of all of this was just the icing on the cake. I wasn't sure what my future employment looked like, but I knew that somehow, I would work alongside my husband. I left working at SCA after we married and was moved to the marketing department at church. It was a much quieter role and involved some graphic design work updating the church newsletter and helping manage our ads in various Christian publications across Australia. I had both loves in one job: admin and design!

Now Matt was running multiple companies and dabbling in publishing when news came through that *Alive* magazine was closing its doors. Not knowing the impact this would have on us personally, I mentioned this to him and what began was a 15 year journey into Christian publishing and media.

The baptism of fire
Our foray into this new business was challenging. By this stage, I had left working at the church (good-bye weekly pay packet) to focus on Initiate Media. Matt believed we needed to adopt a no-debt strategy in running this business and so we both decided that we would not ask for donations. This was going to be a business built on producing a quality product (which became products) that Christians would pay for.

My role in the company was to be art director. Having few design skills under my belt, I had to produce each issue of *Alive*. It was emotionally taxing, as everything fell on my shoulders and I had quite a few teary conversations with the printer about how to produce high quality images and type. My few short design courses were just not enough so I had to learn on the job... and fast.

We worked hard. So hard. In fact, I don't believe I have ever had such an all-consuming role. Many many nights were spent printing, folding and stuffing subscription letters and I sweated blood trying to produce a beautiful looking magazine each issue. We added Ark House Press to our Initiate Media family and to date have published over 500 titles. We were in a glory phase of our business that saw us move from a small office in Mona Vale to a much larger space in Belrose. We employed quite a lot of staff members to assist in advertising sales, reception work, customer service, accounts and even graphic design (to assist me). The office smelt of freshly brewed coffee and there was a great atmosphere of camaraderie between our staff. Times were good!

When the Global Financial Crisis hit us in 2009, it was gut-wrenching. I was heavily pregnant with our third child and one by one, we had to let staff go. The once bustling office was becoming a place of uncertainty for those left. Matt was sending me into the office as he was having to be 'bad cop' with the staff and quite frankly it completely knocked the wind out of his sails. As a visionary and a leader, his job was to pre-empt disaster. But this tidal wave came from nowhere and we were all drowning...

But God

I do love the 'but' of God. His ways are always higher than our ways and when you seek Him, He will give you the answers you need. Matt carved a prayer walk near our house during this time. Our trusty labrador, Lewis, walked beside him as a faithful friend does and he poured his heart out to God. Those prayer walks saved us. Matt turned to God instead of alcohol or substance abuse or worse… That just goes to show you what an incredible man he is. God answered him during those nights of suffering and he came home with renewed hope after one such walk. God had given him a 'digital' strategy for our business.

Matt shared the vision with me and I was on board. I am not always 'on-board', mind you. I do provide a pretty down-the-line sounding board, so when I am in, I am in! This sounded like an amazing God-strategy for our business. So with our loyal team, we made major changes and got to work on building a digital business, thankfully backed by some strong print revenue to keep paying the bills. Sometimes in life you need to stop and regroup. We needed to regroup without heavy overheads. We needed to work out how this digital strategy was going to benefit our readers and the greater Christian community and at the same time remunerate us for our hard work.

A new chapter

I love the thought that our life is a big book and each chapter is a new beginning. It still makes sense in the whole story, but new chapters are exciting. Our move to an almost fully digital business (Ark House Press is still going strong in print) has been a long slow process, but like a tree, it takes years to grow and mature. We have so many exciting projects coming up, including a new branch on the *Christian Woman* tree, but I am so thankful and grateful that God is with us and when we abide in Him, He guides and leads.

Final note: Life with an entrepreneur

If you have ever known an entrepreneur or even been married to one, you'll know that they are wired differently. The world is their oyster and they want to leave a legacy. They write notes and ideas on anything (Matt has napkins and toilet paper with notes on them!) so it's not forgotten… Even at 2am, when the rest of us are sleeping, they are dreaming wide awake. They are the eccentric ones; the ones who think outside of the box. The ones who believe they can make a difference. The passionate and the purposeful. Life is *NOT Business As Usual* for them. To know them is to love them. To do life with them is an epic adventure. It's not always wonderful. It's hard to see some dreams crushed and others blossom, but the ground on which they walk is ever-changing. If you can keep up, then I promise you, you will have a very colourful life.

HAVE MATT DANSWAN SPEAK TO YOUR GROUP

While Initiate Media more than keeps me busy, an important part of my life is talking to people face to face. Be it business groups, churches or at conferences, sharing business foundations and strategies for life success is ultimately what gives me the most joy.

As long as your event is between 1am and 5am in the morning, when I have my spare time, I am free. Just kidding. We have a great team making our business work, and this frees me up to travel and share with others.

Faith is the core of my business and life, as is seeing people move into their destinies.

If you're with a church or conference and you'd like to get in touch, then please visit www.mattdanswan.com and click on the Speaking tab.

One of our team will respond to you within 24 hours.

If you'd like to purchase bulk copies, please contact us at www.

mattdanswan.com.

INSPIRED BUSINESS LIVE

We are launching an exciting new business conference for Christians called Inspired Business Live.

Essentially it is set up to empower Christians in business. Inspired Business Live is not just a 'flowery' conference either. We bring together great minds; business people who can open you up to new ways of doing business.

I am passionate about ensuring there is a robust mix of faith and business. Too much spirituality and everyone is floating around the room, with no practical ideas to take to take away and back to work.

Too much practical and Christians don't realize just what they have in their possession. So this conference is a great mix. If Christian men and women realized just what they have in terms of the power of God, then together we can change the world.

And that's what Inspired Business Live is all about.

Visit www.inspiredbusinesslive.com to learn more.

THE *YOU* ECONOMY

It sounds egotistical and self-centered, but it's so far from the case. Welcome to *The YOU Economy*. In an age where jobs are being sent off-shore, where corporate jobs are becoming increasingly scarce, and where part-time work rules, this book aims to help the non-entrepreneur to become one.

It's also called the 'gig economy'. It's time to embrace it, as it is the future of the western workforce. In America alone, a third of the working population are working in this new economy. They're being forced to mix together short-term jobs, contract work and freelance assignments to make a living.

While this can create a lot of additional income, it also comes with the stress of an uncertain pay packet, as well as being forced to understand a new way of budgeting, allowing for taxation challenges, and more.

In *The YOU Economy*, author Matt Danswan will help you understand your skillset, and from there package together a business model that will help you market yourself and your business to the business world.

Whether your desire is to start your own fully-fledged business, or simply contract yourself out to other companies, *The YOU Economy* will help make your idea a reality.

www.ingramcontent.com/pod-product-compliance
Lightning Source LLC
Chambersburg PA
CBHW022103090426
42743CB00008B/699